On Penalties

ON PENALTIES

Andrew Anthony

YELLOW JERSEY PRESS
LONDON

Published by Yellow Jersey Press 2001

2 4 6 8 10 9 7 5 3 1

Copyright © Andrew Anthony 2000

First published in Great Britain in 2000 by
Yellow Jersey Press
Random House, 20 Vauxhall Bridge Road,
London SW1V 2SA

Random House Australia (Pty) Limited
20 Alfred Street, Milsons Point, Sydney,
New South Wales 2061, Australia

Random House New Zealand Limited
18 Poland Road, Glenfield,
Auckland 10, New Zealand

Random House (Pty) Limited
Endulini, 5A Jubilee Road, Parktown, 2193, South Africa

The Random House Group Limited Reg. No. 954009
www.randomhouse.co.uk

A CIP catalogue record for this book
is available from the British Library

ISBN 0 224 06116 X

Papers used by Random House are natural,
recyclable products made from wood grown in sustainable
forests; the manufacturing processes conform to the
environmental regulations of the country of origin

Typeset by SX Composing DTP, Rayleigh, Essex
Printed and bound in Denmark by
Nørhaven A/S Viborg

'Tragedy ought really to be a great kick at misery.'

D.H. Lawrence

'The difficult thing is that I can't do anything about it now.'

Gareth Southgate

To Isabel

Author's Note

Writing a book is not unlike taking a penalty. OK, there are some differences – a book requires a little more time and also you get to sit down – but there is one important similarity: although both pursuits are solitary, they draw on team support. With that thought, I'd like to thank a number of people for their generous help. In no particular order: BBC Sports, which kindly allowed me access to its videotapes of matches and interviews, and specifically, Jo McCusker, for her most welcome aid and advice; Gary Dowden, an extraordinary fount of football statistics, who can be reached at www.footiemad.demon. co.uk; Bob Wilson for his time and thoughts; Dr George Sik, for his foolhardy bravery in daring to peek inside the footballer's mind; and Mark Crossley, formerly of Nottingham Forest FC, who stood up large.

For information, I most often referred to Clark Miller's *He Always Puts It To The Right*, Glenn Hoddle's *My World Cup Story* and Tony Adams's *Addicted*. My appreciation extends also to various colleagues at the *Observer*, most obviously everyone on the sports desk, and the editors who allowed me the space to get the book written. Thanks to Louise Chunn for her understanding, if not of penalties, then of everything else. And I am especially grateful to Rachel Cugnoni, the originator and editor of this book, for her unstinting encouragement and astute observation. Finally, I should also like to record my debt to, and respect for, all the players who have been prepared to put themselves on the penalty spot, without whom, literally, this book could not have been written.

Needless to add, if I fail to hit the target, the responsibility is entirely my own.

Andrew Anthony, London 2000

On Penalties

CHAPTER ONE

The Indecision Is Final

The penalty, is it a metaphor for the indecision of modern life or simply an easy way of scoring a goal? I think it's safe to assume that this question was not in the forefront of David Batty's mind when he walked up to take his ill-conceived penalty against Argentina in the 1998 World Cup. Certainly, there was nothing in the imperviously stoic demeanour of the Yorkshireman to suggest that he viewed that penalty shoot-out as anything but a penalty shoot-out. Whatever it meant to Batty, it wasn't a workshop on existential doubt. His later comments regarding his thinking at the time would seem to confirm that he tended towards the 'just stick it in the back of the net' approach. 'I were really confident,' he explained some months afterwards. 'I said to Shearer in the centre circle: "I'm gonna blast it down the middle."' Those are not the words

1

of a man who was burdened by the unbearable weight of symbolism.

There were other burdens, of course, the kind that even a Yorkshireman would find hard to ignore: history, responsibility, the sheer expectant mass of the watching world. Compelling factors, yet they don't quite explain why Batty missed. In particular, they fail to account for why he changed his mind. Come the moment, he attempted to place the ball, rather than 'blast' it, and for the third time inside a decade the England team lost a major international penalty shoot-out.

Roberto Baggio, the sublimely pony-tailed Italian who fluffed a penalty in the 1994 World Cup final shoot-out, once said that there is only one way you can guarantee not to miss a penalty and that is not to take one. In the same vein, the obvious answer to why Batty missed is that Carlos Roa, the Argentinian goalkeeper, saved his shot. The man himself, I imagine, would appreciate that sort of blunt logic. To reduce the penalty to this simple exchange, however, is to miss something vital, aside from the goal.

The appeal of the penalty lies ostensibly in its orchestrated suspense. We know something is going to happen but we don't know what it will be. For this reason some critics have found the penalty shoot-out, which is the main focus of this book, a contrived drama, an absurd ordeal. One sportswriter compared it to bad art. To him it was no better than cheap melodrama. No doubt there is an element of melodrama in shoot-outs, especially when they are truly gripping, but it is rarely cheap melodrama – if only because failure comes at such a price. I would go so far as to say that the shoot-out is as near perfect an allegory of the human condition as sport offers. Of course, the field is rich in experiential metaphors, with all the triumphs and disasters, winners and losers, and count-less other stupefying clichés that make up the world of competitive games. The beauty of the penalty, though, is that it powerfully represents the fear and the hope, and the regret or relief, that are compressed into the meaningful junctures of life.

The football penalty is unique in sport because of the emphasis it places on conscious choice. For a brief period the game stops and the penalty-taker enters his own chamber of truth, a place where actions have ineluctable consequences. The penalty shoot-out goes even further. In its combination of individual choice and collective responsibility it attains an almost moral significance. If that sounds a little pretentious, or possibly more than a little, then think about how things usually work in competitive games.

Sport is largely an intuitive endeavour which rewards honed instinct. Even in a non-reactive game like golf, the four-foot putt (the nearest golfing equivalent to a football penalty) only really provides one successful option – the ball following a certain line into the hole – and there are no active variables, such as a goalkeeper. You just have to hit the target. Similarly, penalties in rugby and basketball are relatively straightforward affairs with minimal variations. With a football penalty, though, the taker is confronted with a genuine decision. And that presents a distinct problem.

The metaphysics of the penalty were first explored by Peter Handke. His novel, *Die Angst des Tormanns beim Elfmeter* or *The Goalie's Anxiety at the Penalty Kick*, was published in 1970, the year that penalty shoot-outs were introduced to an indifferent world. Fittingly, it was a German film director, Wim Wenders, who took up the idea in his 1971 adaptation of Handke, *The Goalkeeper's Fear of the Penalty*. I say fittingly because Wenders's countrymen have excelled at the penalty's physics ever since, with one notable exception. The West German national side lost the final of the 1976 European Nations Cup, as the competition was then known, in a shoot-out. Subsequently, the Germans have won four major shoot-outs in which, put together, they have missed just one solitary penalty kick.

Still, I doubt that German footballers have studied Wenders's contribution. And I'm certain their English counterparts share this aesthetic oversight. At least I don't recall mention of Wenders in those questionnaires *Shoot* magazine used to run back in the 1970s (favourite food: steak and chips; most difficult opponent: the wife; favourite type of film: New German Cinema). Yet, while the lugubrious German may have been slightly oblique, he had some intriguing things to say about the nature of the penalty.

His film tells the story of a disaffected goalkeeper who travels around, radiating ineffable despair. He is called Bloch: his job is to block but his life seems also depressingly blocked. (German football often throws up these names that appear unfeasibly blessed with meaning. Look, for example, at that of the player who would do for England in Euro '96: Kuntz.) Killing time, notably by casually murdering a young woman he seduces, Bloch eventually ends up watching a nondescript football game. Out of the blue, he initiates a conversation with another spectator, a travelling salesman who, this being a study in alienation, is just passing through. Bloch asks the rep if he has ever tried to watch the beleaguered goalkeeper rather than the attackers with the ball. The rep shakes his head. 'It's hard to drag your eyes from the forward to the goalkeeper,' explains Bloch. 'Instead of the ball, you see the goalkeeper dodging back and forth and shouting at the defenders. Usually, you only notice him when the ball's shot at the goal. It's funny to see the goalkeeper without the ball, waiting for it.'

The salesman attempts to keep his eyes on the goalkeeper. 'I can't watch for that long,' he complains. 'I keep looking back to the forwards. It's like squinting. When a man goes to the door, you don't watch the handle. Your head aches. You can't breathe.'

'You get used to it,' says Bloch.

It's a curious scene, quietly disturbing, bleakly ironic. The most obvious irony, the invisibility of the goalkeeper, is underlined in the following scene when a penalty is given. For in a penalty setting the goalkeeper becomes suddenly and conspicuously apparent. Now we all watch the handle and not the door. It is, if anyone's, the penalty-taker's head that aches and it is he who cannot breathe. In this sense, as has often been stated, the goalkeeper need have no fear of the penalty. He is not expected to save the penalty so therefore he retains a psychological edge over his opponent, who is expected to score. However, the uneven duel between attacker and keeper exerts a more complex rivalry than merely that between underdog and favourite. An extraordinary mental dance of second- and third- and even fourth-guessing is choreographed in seconds.

Here is Bloch again, responding to the award of the spot-kick: 'A penalty! The goalkeeper wonders into which corner it will go. If he knows the opposing player, he knows the kicker's favourite corner, but the kicker knows he knows. So the goalkeeper wonders if he might choose the other corner this time. But the kicker knows that, too, so maybe he'll go for his favourite. And so on and so on.'

Footballers have many impressive qualities

– bravery, stamina, determination – but decision-making, like verbal eloquence, is seldom one of them. It's simply not something they're used to doing. Their lives are determined by trained response and skilled reflex. The choices players make on the pitch – run or mark, shoot or pass, elbow or headbutt – are nothing more than micro-decisions, instant reactions, impulses. Real decisions, big decisions, the kind that demand or, worse, *afford* time and thought, are something to be taken care of by the manager, or the agent, the adviser or the wife. Footballers themselves don't have a lot to do with them. Now, don't misunderstand me, that isn't a criticism. Who can blame them? Who wants to make decisions if they can be avoided? I mention this psychic aversion with all the humility and sympathy of a man who would rather find out what's on Sky Sports 3 than come to a firm decision about almost anything. Decision-making, if we are honest, is a mournfully oppressive business. The human spirit may crave freedom, but it recoils from choice. To commit to one option – to live with a certain person rather than another, say, or to go to this New Year's Eve party and not that one – is to confront the irreversibility of time. In this sense, to make a choice in life is to recognise the inevitability of death. That's why we procrastinate, or attempt to suspend the moment of decision, for as long as we can. And frequently longer if we happen to be male.

The penalty is a graphic illustration of the instant when a decision's postponement is no longer possible. Batty changed his mind, which is another way of delaying a decision, or retaining a notional option, until the last moment. He said he altered his plan because he felt confident. Bobby Robson, who watched his England team lose on penalties to Germany in the 1990 World Cup semi-final, had three golden rules when it came to penalty-taking: (1) Make up your mind; (2) Don't change it; And (3) do what's in your head. Robson is a likeable man who is England's second most successful manager, but his thoughts have not always been predicated on what logicians call sound reasoning. Numbers one and two follow but number three only works if what's in your head as you run up to the ball is the same as the decision you've made. With Batty numbers one and three didn't tally, so where did that leave number two? Many footballers attempt to negate this mental mess by not making a decision, by simply choosing to kick the ball, violently, in the general direction of the goal. But, of course, that in itself is a decision.

The penalty allows no get-out clauses. It's make-your-mind-up time. There is no going back. Do or die. The very finality of the act is what, I feel, inspires the spectator's near morbid fascination for the penalty. When it first arrived in the nineteenth century, it was nicknamed the 'death penalty'. And what do we call that stage of a penalty shoot-out when whoever misses loses? Sudden death. Does all this sound a little extreme? It's just a game, as people say when they lose, nobody really dies. Well, nobody physically expires, drops dead from the stress, but there are plenty who seem to have died a *little* in the process. Look, for example, at the *petit mort* of Denis Bergkamp. At his best, Bergkamp is a dangerously spectral presence, able to slip into the goalmouth almost unnoticed. When he missed the last-minute penalty in the 1999 FA Cup semi-final against arch rivals Manchester United, Bergkamp appeared a ghost haunted by himself, imprisoned in a past moment. The instant Peter Schmeichel parried the ball away, the blood seemed to drain from Bergkamp's already anaemic-looking face. And I'm not certain his game has yet regained its sanguine purpose.

Not everyone's pain is quite so manifest. When Stuart Pearce missed his penalty in that 1990 World Cup semi-final, it was clear that he wasn't happy. You knew that he wouldn't be disco dancing later that night. But the depth of his suffering was impossible to fathom even, one suspects, for Pearce himself. It was not until six years later, against Spain in the quarter-final shoot-out of Euro '96 that we learned what had really happened to the steely left-back fondly known as Psycho. Something buried in his soul had indeed died that sad night in Turin. How did we know? Because it came frighteningly back to life at Wembley, like some demonic rebirth. I shall, of course, return to that supercharged incident. For the moment, it's enough to say that the penalty calls for a premeditated decision; and the wrong decision carries its own, often more severe, penalty.

Is that a bad thing? As well as standing accused of vulgar theatricality, the penalty shoot-out has also been deemed unfair. The French midfield player Christian Karembeu was widely quoted when he criticised the shoot-out after his team had defeated Holland in the quarter-final of Euro '96. His friend and Sampdoria teammate, Clarence Seedorf, had missed the vital penalty for the Dutch. 'It is loading a bullet into the chamber of a gun,' said Karembeu, 'and asking everyone to pull the trigger. Someone will get the bullet, you know that. And it will reduce them to nothing. Fair? Fairness is not even an issue.'

In fairness, fairness plays roughly the same role in sport as love does in sex. It's nice if it's there, but it's not essential for entertainment. The enjoyment of the penalty shoot-out lies precisely in its seemingly random allotment of joy and anguish. Cruel and arbitrary, it is everything that we profess to disdain in sport but secretly relish. Much has been made of the intolerable psychological pressure, yet the complaints, with the honourable exception of Karembeu, come almost universally from the losing side. Victory, as ever, validates all.

The semi-final of Euro '96 was a particularly unkind experience, if you were not German. It is widely agreed, in England at least, that England did not deserve to lose to Germany on penalties because they had been the better side in the preceding 120 minutes of open play. This may be true but they were plainly not the better side during the 120 minutes of open play against Spain in the previous round, and few English supporters resented winning on penalties in that game. You would spend a long time searching through south-east London before you found a Charlton fan who felt his team should not have been promoted to the Premiership in 1998. The fact is that Sunderland, whom Charlton defeated 7-6 on penalties in the final of the First Division play-offs, were by all other measurable criteria a far superior side. But if you start discussing fairness in this context you might just as well ban last-minute goals or deflected goals or unintentional goals.

Come that legendary football hour, at the end of the day, shoot-outs are no more unjust than all the other might-have-beens and nearly-weres that go to make up any game of sport. They merely provide a more defined means by which players, fans and managers can delude themselves. Take, by way of example, the words of Martin O'Neil, the excitable former Leicester manager, spoken after his team's triumph over Leeds in the fourth round of the Worthington Cup in 1999. 'This was a big, big performance by us,' he said proudly, 'a monster effort to beat that side.' You might think he was referring to a gutsy fight-back from two-goals down but the score was 0-0 at full-time, as indeed it was after extra-time. Leicester won 4-2 on penalties. Monster effort.

But what's the alternative? A replay of the fourth round of the Worthington Cup? Then a second replay? People have lives to live. Those who deride shoot-outs have no workable answers. Play on until one side scores? An idea that conjures up the appalling scenario of the six-hour deadlock. One-against-one from the centre circle? A poor man's penalty shoot-out. Tony Banks, the former Minister for Sport, once argued that shoot-outs had been 'a terrible innovation'. Taking into account the number of free kicks and corners was, he suggested, a preferable solution. He thought that even tossing a coin, which used to happen in European games prior to 1970, was better because shoot-outs unfairly favoured successful sides. 'The big-team players', he explained, 'are more used to the nerve-racking atmosphere of big-time football.' You can see his point. He might also have added that skilful players have an unreasonable advantage over technically limited players. The shoot-out works. Its only fault is that it might work too well.

Among the many extraordinary things that a game of football can be, one of them, alas, is extraordinarily boring. I can't say for certain, but I suspect that there has yet to be a boring shoot-out. The danger here might be that the game itself becomes overshadowed by its artificial ending, especially as television coverage continues to grow. Penalties, apart from the havoc they reek on schedules, are innately televisual. They are in many ways better suited to the claustrophobic dimensions of the box than they are to the wide-angle perspective from the stands. Pitch-side, shoot-outs can seem forlorn affairs, especially when viewed from the wrong end of the stadium. There is the bonus of being able to watch the drama in the round – the players grouped in the centre circle, and the lonely walk up to the penalty spot – but the overall effect within a stadium is one of detached unreality. In true postmodern style, it's more real on TV. The fashionable view inside football holds that television, with all its money and glitz, is a sinister influence. Could the hyperbole that televised penalties generate dim the TV audience's appreciation of the finer points of the game – the puff and slog, the kick and chase? Surely it's the intractable saga of open play that creates the necessary preconditions for a shoot-out: the exhaustion, the frazzled nerves, the pressing need, for the viewer at least, to visit the lavatory. Removed from its context, the shoot-out would lose its meaning, not to mention its metaphorical power.

A more conceivable drawback in the pro-liferation of shoot-outs is that teams will learn to play for them. Instead of attempting to win through traditional means – scoring more goals than their opponents – they'll defend a goalless draw and snatch victory in the ensuing shoot-out. Steaua Bucharest were accused of this ploy when they played against Terry Venables's Barcelona in the final of the European Cup, as it then was, back in 1986. Five years later Red Star Belgrade were said to have pulled the same trick against Marseille in the final of the same competition. And Argentina stood charged on much the same count in the 1990 World Cup. What do all these teams have in common? We didn't like them. Steaua were the wretched Romanian dictator Ceausescu's military side. And although the Eastern bloc had collapsed by

1991, teams like Red Star, which were once unfailingly described as 'crack', had become known in the West as 'cynical'. Argentina were asking for it. They were always asking for it. Yet Liverpool were hailed as great tacticians when they nicked a 1-1 draw against Roma in the final of the 1984 European Cup, and then won on penalties. Anyway, if Steaua, for example, had made themselves penalty robots why did they miss two in the shoot-out (Barcelona missed all of theirs)? How can you guarantee winning on penalties? If there is a way, why haven't other teams picked up on it? Why hasn't someone told Gareth Southgate?

Southgate, you will recall, hit the second-worst penalty of all time to ease England out of Euro '96. Three and half years later, on the same historic evening that Leicester trounced Leeds with that monster effort, Southgate hit the worst penalty of all time. In a shoot-out against West Ham, in the fourth round of the Worthington Cup, he stepped up to strike a penalty, but instead rolled a back pass to Shaka Hislop, the West Ham keeper. Hislop didn't save the ball so much as pick it up. It was the fourth penalty Southgate had taken in his career. He had also missed the previous three.

ON PENALTIES

How difficult is it to convert a penalty? At the outset of this chapter I asked if the penalty was simply an easy way of scoring a goal. You may have noticed that the question remains, in essence, unanswered. The neglect is partly due to my suspicion that the most interesting thing about penalties is not what they are but what they represent – the psychodynamics of the decision. It's also because there is no secret to penalty-taking, no hidden technique. The mental trauma may be concealed – although there are plenty of facial and bodily 'tells' as to the taker's state of mind and confidence – but in terms of physical action, what you see is what you get. And it's not hard to get. There's the ball, there's the goal, there's the goalkeeper. You just have to put the first bit into the second while avoiding the third. The theory is straightforward.

In practice, which is to say not in practice but in a proper game, Diego Maradona, Michel Platini, Zico and Roberto Baggio, to name just four of the finest players in history, have all missed from the penalty spot at the very highest level. These are men who, on the turn, with three defenders bearing down on them, could land a ball from sixty yards at exactly the right spot so that a striker would not have to break stride to meet it. They are the kind of players who could keep a grapefruit airborne all day with their feet, and could probably peel and serve one in the same manner if requested. So let's take a moment to consider the physical dimensions of the penalty.

From a distance of thirty-six feet, a penalty-taker has roughly 180 square feet of space at which to aim. Taking the target as a whole, twenty-four feet wide by eight feet high, there are in fact 192 square feet in which to place to the ball, but that doesn't allow for approximately twelve square feet of mobile goalkeeper. If the ball is struck very firmly, let's say at the speed of sixty miles per hour, it would travel at eighty-eight feet per second. That leaves the goalkeeper much less than half a second in which to respond. A more common velocity is between forty and fifty miles per hour. Even so, the keeper still has no more than half a second to cover 192 square feet. Which is to say, in the time it took you to read 'Which is to say', he would have to launch his body to the correct area of the target.

'It's very close when you're standing there,' said Bob Wilson, the former Arsenal keeper turned TV pundit who is also the England number one David Seaman's goalkeeping coach. 'If you walk out in the cold light of day in the stadium with no one around and you put the ball on the spot and you stand facing the goal, you seriously think, well, it's impossible to miss.'

Of the seventy-one penalties awarded in the FA Premiership in 1998–1999, only fifty were scored. Twenty-one, or just under thirty per cent, were apparently not impossible to miss.

With these figures in mind, I motored out one morning to Bob's home just beyond the M25 in the mock-Tudor world of Hertfordshire, a place that is to footballers what Salt Lake City is to Mormons. My motives for the visit were twofold. I wanted to talk to Bob about penalties in his own capacity as a former pro and informed commentator. And more than that, I wanted to engage his help in setting up a mini-contest with Seaman in which I could test my own penalty-taking abilities against arguably the world's best. I aimed to take ten penalties against him. It wouldn't matter, for the purposes of my small experiment, if the encounter took place at an empty training ground after the other players had left. In fact, the fewer distractions, the more cut-off from external 'pressures', the better. I simply wanted to see how technically difficult it was to beat a keeper of Seaman's ability from twelve yards. I hadn't kicked a ball in anger for a couple of years and even then I was no more than an average Sunday league player. How many out of ten would I find it impossible not to score?

Bob, to his immense credit, immediately warmed to the idea and promised to sell it to Seaman at their next coaching session. In the meantime, we got down to discussing the penalty, a subject on which Bob, as mild-mannered in person as he is on air, held some uncharacteristically trenchant views. 'What really needles me', he said suddenly, as he wrenched a teabag out from his mug, 'is that when I was a kid I used to see penalties retaken all the time for the goalkeeper moving too early. I can't remember the last time I saw a penalty retaken for a goalkeeper moving too early.'

Not recently for sure. I dimly recall Martin Peters, playing for Tottenham in the early seventies, retaking a penalty twice against, I think, Norwich, because the referee had deemed that the goalkeeper had twice moved prematurely. Nowadays, I can't conceive of what a goalkeeper would have to do for the kick to be taken again. Stand on the edge of the six-yard box? Slide tackle the kicker? Given the zeal and severity with which referees currently deal with just about any other infraction of the rules, it is a little mysterious that they allow goalkeepers such latitude with the penalty law. The law changed in 1997, it's true – goalkeepers were allowed to move along their line before the ball was hit – but then it has changed a number of times since its introduction on 2 June 1891.

William McCrum, the wealthy son of the High Sheriff for County Armagh in Ireland, first suggested the idea of a penalty to the Irish FA in 1890. The owner of a linen factory and a keen cricketer, McCrum was also, of course, a goalkeeper. As Peter Shilton would write almost a century later: 'A penalty kick is usually a moment of high drama in a match and an interesting situation for a keeper . . . There are few better feelings in football at any level than saving a penalty.' Back in the late nineteenth century, football, which was in its youth as an organised sport, was essentially a free-for-all. Managers frequently complain nowadays about players being prevented from showing their natural aggression. There were few problems of this nature in McCrum's era. As a defensive tactic, manslaughter was not unheard of. A favoured rearguard action of the period entailed defenders jumping up and kneeing their opponents in the stomach. As well as the swiftness with which it brought attacks to a stop, this challenge was also highly effective at rupturing intestines. In his book *He Always Puts It To The Right*, Clark Miller quotes from the report of a trial in Leicestershire in which it emerged that two players from a team called Enderby died as a result of over-enthusiastic tackling.

Even so, there was great opposition to any rules that were seen to curtail the freedom of expression of defenders. McCrum's suggestion was initially met with disapproval, but after a year of negotiations the International Football Board instituted the new ruling, which was quite limited in its remit.

If any player shall intentionally trip or hold an opposing player, or deliberately handle the ball within 12 yards from his own goal-line, the referee shall, on appeal, award the opposing side a penalty kick, to be taken from any point 12 yards from the goal-line, under the following conditions:

All players, with the exception of the player taking the penalty kick and the opposing goalkeeper (who shall not advance more than six yards from the goal-line), shall stand at least six yards behind the ball. The ball shall be in play when the kick is taken, and a goal may be scored from the penalty kick.

You could, naturally, still elbow or kick or push or charge your opponent without fear of incurring a penalty. The other four points to notice about the wording are that there was no set penalty spot, the penalty area was twelve yards not eighteen yards and extended to both touchlines, goalkeepers were able to come out to six yards and the penalty was not a mandatory award for a foul in the penalty area but one that was gained on appeal to the referee.

In its early days the penalty was unpopular among many players who viewed it as a slur on their good sporting conduct. The Corinthians, the renowned gentleman amateurs, were said never to appeal for penalties, nor, apparently, did they defend them, the goalkeeper usually taking the opportunity to light a smoke while leaning against a goal-post. This was the opinion of their legendary captain, C.B. Fry: 'A standing insult to sportsmen to have to play under a rule which assumes that players intend to trip, hack and push opponents and to behave like cads of the most unscrupulous kidney.'

Still, among those penalties that were contested, very often the goalkeeper, who was allowed to rush out, got the better of the exchange. Administrators attempted to redress the balance in favour of the attacker and various amendments were made and clauses added over the years. By 1905, when goal-keepers were stopped from advancing from their goal-line, the law looked very similar to that of today. There was one further major change in 1929, when it was stated that the goalkeeper 'must stand on his own goal-line'. The following year, the word stand was defined. It meant 'that the goalkeeper must not move his feet until the penalty kick has been taken'.

And that's how things stood until August 1997, when goalkeepers were suddenly allowed to move along their goal-line. 'Before then,' said Bob, 'the rule said quite specifically the goalkeeper had to stay on his line and could not move until the ball was kicked; that is, travelled its own circumference.'

Few goalkeepers took notice of this law, especially as, for no recorded reason, referees allowed them to break it with impunity throughout the eighties and nineties. In 1990, an inauspicious year for England and penalty-taking, Charles Hughes, then the FA's chief of coaching, published a book entitled *The Winning Formula*. A crude statistical analysis of football, its main thesis was that teams were most successful when they eschewed complicated passing and kicked the ball long and early. Hughes's thinking on penalties earned just a few paragraphs of space among two hundred pages of facts and figures. Although meagre, his advice to goalkeepers was unmistakably clear. 'It is important that the goalkeeper should not move before the ball is kicked. Not only is this the law of the game, it also helps the goalkeeper make a save.'

Bob was adamant. 'Nobody who ever saved a penalty, or virtually nobody, did it without breaking that rule.' He stood up to illustrate his point. 'Imagine that wall there is one post,' he said, then turned and started walking away from the wall. 'One, two, three,' he called out with each large pace he took. When he got to eight he stopped and shouted back to me, 'I'm actually out of the room now.' How big is a goal? Bigger than Bob Wilson's sitting room. He came back in and stood in the middle of the imaginary space he had created. 'Now you think of the guy there and me here. I stand on my tiptoes and I can touch underneath the bar. It's a *chasm*. It's amazing how that can be made to look difficult.'

But it can.

Bob told me the story of how he learned to save penalties. In 1972, he had been playing in goal for Arsenal for four years without saving a single penalty. He was the goalkeeper when Arsenal won the double in 1971. They did it, though, without Wilson saving a penalty. The following year Alan Ball moved to Arsenal and taught Bob the secret of the penalty.

'Very soon after he arrived,' recalled Bob, 'we were having a training session one day and he was the penalty-taker. This little squeaking voice said, "You see, you're fucking useless at penalties." I said, "what do you know about it? Tell me what's wrong then." '

What an irreligious thrill it is to hear the

avuncular Bob get profane in his language –
but penalties can do that to a man. Ball told
Bob that he made his intention obvious to the
penalty-taker. 'You make your mind up, don't
you.'

'And I did. It was difficult enough goalkeeping, I'd never really studied penalty-
saving. Bally said, "Look if you're a class
player like me, if you go early I just wait and
change my mind." I said, "What do you
suggest?"'

Ball explained that he was sometimes
thrown if a goalkeeper moved his body one
way but then went the other way. 'So he puts
all his balance one way, or at least looks as if
he has, but he keeps his spring together and
dives the other way.'

They started practising together, with Bob
pretending to do the opposite of what he then
did. On Boxing Day, about six weeks after Ball
had brought his attention to his flawed
penalty-saving technique, Bob faced Mick
Channon at the Dell. Channon, an England
international, had not missed a penalty for
four years. He was also a good friend of Ball.

'We're winning one-nil with twenty
minutes to go when they get a penalty. I'm on
my line and I see Bally going, "Remember,

remember." I'm going, "OK, OK." So I make all this movement to my right, and he knocks it to my left. I hurl myself to my left and what happens? I save the penalty. The thing is I blocked it and it's still in the danger area. I'm trying to get up on my feet and Bally is standing there screaming at me, "I told you, I told you." Anyway it went out and we won one-nil.'

English football is a conservative environment. While coaches and players are always looking to gain the edge on their opponents, innovation and change, as foreign coaches have learned here over the last few years, are still viewed with great suspicion. For years the penalty was seen as an unrelated addition to the game, a freak offshoot that demanded no concerted attention. In a sense the idea of the penalty as an unsporting act has never wholly disappeared. Although nobody thinks of it in terms of cheating any more, the notion persists that the penalty is more to do with luck and chance than skill and practice.

Back in 1972, when Bob Wilson was goalkeeper for the best team of the day in the country, there was nothing particularly untoward about the fact that he had no strategy for saving penalties. Gradually, that outlook has evolved into a more serious approach. Now-adays most top-flight keepers maintain lists and details on each team's penalty-takers. But a residue of complacency remains. Thirty years after the arrival of the penalty shoot-out, England has yet to develop a system of training to deal with it. That neglect has cost at least one World Cup and a European Championship. If that situation is to change, and England are to progress, then a methodical analysis of how to score from the spot is urgently required. At the moment, the indecision surrounding penalties is not just metaphorical.

CHAPTER TWO

A Night To Remember

I could tell that Stuart Pearce was going to miss. It was more than a hunch. What I had was a sensory intimation of disaster. The information came first from what I saw but it was another sense that told me something was wrong. You could say it was a sixth sense, although I think I would call it a fashion sense. Those shorts. I knew the second Pearce placed the ball on the spot that no man could score a penalty wearing his shorts that far up his body. God knows, it would have required untold determination just to be able to *walk* in them. They had obviously been adjusted at the conclusion of extra time. But far too enthusiastically. Nerves? He always wore them high back then, of course, but now it was as if they had somehow snagged on the hairs of his armpits.

If, in Cher's memorable phrase, I could turn

31

back time, I would want someone to tug at those shorts to give Pearce the necessary room to move and breathe. But who? What man in his right mind would pull down Psycho's smalls, even in the high jinks of a training session, let alone in the shoot-out for a place in the final of the 1990 World Cup? Gazza, who did not possess a right mind, would have been the sole candidate for the job. Yet he was in no fit state, following the booking that excluded him from the final, to mess with the left-back's Umbros. Gascoigne had been summarily removed from the defining event of his life and had retreated behind his tears into some unreachable corner of his traumatised self.

There was nothing to be done. Pearce was always going to take that kick grievously restricted by the incautious arrangement of his kit. (Incidentally, it wasn't until the following year, in the semi-final of the FA Cup, that Tottenham Hotspur previewed a retro long-short which finally put paid to the high-waist look that was a painful legacy of what passed for style in the seventies. In the final they met Nottingham Forest, who still favoured a snugger fit around the crotch. Spurs won but not before Pearce, sporting his waistband fractionally lower than he did in Turin, scored with a vicious free kick that seemed to scream with his pain.) You can't turn back time. You can only relive it.

The penalty shoot-out is a creature of the video age and the instant action replay. Arriving on 5 August 1970, it evolved alongside televised football, each one influencing the other. The shoot-out showed TV how to dramatise sport and TV turned the shoot-out into a self-conscious event, into a spectacle, into 'live' TV. As if watching himself on a screen, each player envisions what he is about to do before doing it and then relives the moment as soon as he has finished. There is, among both viewer and player, a heightened awareness of time suspended, and a daunting sense of the future impatiently waiting to have its say. Such is the level of anticipation that you almost feel as though you are watching the replay before it happens. It's not necessary to be an England supporter to apprehend a powerful sense of *déjà vu* as a shoot-out unfolds, although it probably helps. It's almost as if every player knows his role – the superconfident expert, the lucky chancer, the doomed loser – and is destined to enact it. Each penalty feels rehearsed but, it would appear, never practised. Then someone misses and the extended present suddenly stops and the future, with all its immutable consequences, rushes in. Unless you're the one who misses. In which case you're stuck on rewind and replay, rewind and replay, rewind and replay. That's the penalty.

If you're going to do something that you might not be able to forget, why not make it an experience you might want to remember? That was the line of thinking that Antonin Panenka appeared to adopt in 1976. Like a character out of a Milan Kundera novel, Panenka wanted to make a penalty into a statement. He wasn't overtly political but then you didn't need to be to attract trouble in Czechoslovakia in the mid-seventies. His subversion lay in the idea you could transform a regimented, rigid task – like taking a penalty – into something different and unexpected and meaningful. 'Usually before going to bed,' Panenka recently recalled, 'I would think hard about how to invent a penalty kick that would beat a goalkeeper.' And, he might have added, one that would beat the system.

When Czechoslovakia met West Germany in Belgrade in the 1976 final of the European

A NIGHT TO REMEMBER

Nations Cup, the Czech team was much stronger than the side that lost to Germany at Wembley in the same competition twenty years later. Panenka had dreamed the night before the game that he would take a penalty that would decide the match. But Czechoslovakia, who had already beaten England, the USSR and Holland, went two-up after twenty-five minutes and looked like they were about to record their first triumph in a major international tournament. The Germans, not untypically, came back and scored an equaliser with a minute left on the clock. There were no goals in extra time and the game went to penalties for the first time in international football. The first seven penalties were converted and the Czechs led 4-3 when Uli Hoeness blasted the ball over the bar. The next player in line for Czechoslovakia was Panenka. All he had to do to become a national hero and register his country's name in football history was score from the penalty spot.

In 1976 – in the middle of the Brezhnev years in the Eastern bloc – Czechoslovakia was not a place in which to mock authority or to send up the collective will with an act of flagrant individualism. In Kundera's novel

ON PENALTIES

The Joke, the hero is sent to a labour camp for writing a silly legend – 'Optimism is the opium of the people ... long live Trotsky' – on a postcard to his girlfriend. Panenka was about to deliver perhaps a more seditious message, and not to his girlfriend but to tens of millions of viewers across Europe and, specifically, back home in Czechoslovakia. 'I got this idea that on the run up to the ball I could make the goalie think that I wanted to place the ball to the post but at the very last moment I would just chip it so that the ball would descend very slowly into the middle of the goal ... I had told our goalie, Ivor Viktor, of my plan the night before,' said Panenka. 'But he said: "No, no, don't do it. It's too arrogant. What if you fail?"'

Viktor could not have imagined that the notional penalty would turn out to be so crucial. All the same, Panenka ignored his goalkeeper's advice. From outside the penalty box, he began a long run up. A couple of steps from the ball, he opened his body, his left arm swinging out in preparation, and at the next step, Sepp Maier, the German goalkeeper, started towards his left. Panenka launched his right foot at the ball, then slowed it just as it was about to make contact, so that it merely kissed the ball. The ball looped towards the centre of the goal, as if in slow motion, and dropped gently, like a small cushion, into the back of the net, with Maier sprawled helplessly by his left-hand post.

People have asked Panenka what would have happened if he had missed, if Maier had just stood there and casually let the ball fall into his outstretched arms? 'I'd probably have spent the last twenty-five years as a factory worker,' is Panenka's throwaway reply. 'I don't think the Communists would have been too pleased with me. They might have accused me of ridiculing their system.'

The world had changed, or was changing, when England lined up against West Germany in Turin's Stadio degli Alpi on the night of Tuesday 4 July 1990. Three days earlier Chancellor Helmut Kohl had announced monetary union between East and West Germany and all border controls were lifted for the first time in forty-five years. The Berlin Wall had been down for some months and the Eastern bloc was in a state of collapse. But full unification between the two Germanys had not yet been completed and so it was still West Germany (East Germany having not made it to the finals) that England met on that benighted evening in Turin.

It was, I recall, unbearably hot and sticky. By extra time I couldn't take it any longer. I wasn't perspiring so much as expiring. I knew that I would have to take urgent and extreme action and I spoke to the other people I was with to see what they were thinking. They agreed that something ought to be done. So I got up and opened the windows. I was reluctant to do so because I lived at the beginning of the A1 in Archway, north London, and the noise of the lorries outside was such that it rendered John Motson's commentary even more incomprehensible than usual. But the room was overheated with agitation and, anyway, the traffic had subsided, dispersed to TV sets across the country. London was dead because our hopes were still alive.

Which means that I wasn't in Turin. This is not a tour-of-duty memoir. There are no tales of unwashed underwear in a Cagliari campsite, no sordid recollections of espresso jags in Naples. I had only ever been a passive follower of England. The football itself, invariably dour and insipid, was enough to discourage active support. (What happened to players when they put on an England shirt? Why did they look so *tired*?) And there were plenty of other disincentives: Wembley was a slag-heap of a venue which, contrary to its myth, desperately lacked atmosphere; that inane national anthem; the strange people who *did* follow England – bitter men from places like Stevenage and Warrington, cretins, Nazis, sociopaths and the sullen ranks of the silent majority grumbling quietly to themselves. There was none of the wit or unity that you could find in club football, no real shared sense of purpose. With away games – i.e., in *foreign* lands – the situation was far worse. The percentage of demented misfits seemed to leap terrifyingly upwards. I was never sure if it was the joyless football that attracted this miserable collection of Little Ing-ger-lunders or vice versa. Perhaps it was a symbiotic process. Either way, no sane adult needed to be involved.

So there I was in Archway in the shadow, not of the Italian Alps, but of the DHSS tower. In fact, a comparatively small group of English fans attended the Stadio degli Alpi that July night. Only 2,000 tickets had been officially allocated to English fans, who had been led on a frenzied tarantella from Sardinia to Bologna and on to Naples, before arriving in Turin. Estimates put the real figure inside at as little as 4,000. The Germans, by contrast, who had a small distance to travel from the Bavarian border, numbered some 40,000. During the first round, the English, inevitably, had excited the attentions of the local police in Cagliari, where it was reported that bars were smashed up and bricks were thrown. England had only just emerged from a bleak decade that included Heysel and Hillsborough, a dark period in which Margaret Thatcher's government had deemed football politically unacceptable. The world and, in particular, the *caribinieri*, were waiting to pounce on any manifestation of the English problem.

In Turin the English made a good deal of noise, given their limited number, and were in especially ebullient vocal form with the chant: 'What's it like to lose a war?' Yet it was the Germans who behaved most shamefully. They booed and made ape-like sounds every time one of England's two black players, Paul Parker and Des Walker, touched the ball. In addition, the German players themselves were less than sporting. Jurgen Klinsmann, 'like so many of his countrymen, appears to have a low resistance to pain,' was how Christopher Davies of the *Daily Tele-*

graph drily noted the ease with which the Germans went to ground when tackled. Klinsmann's strike partner, Rudi Voller, exemplified the team's charmless arrogance. 'We know we are better than England,' he said prior to the semi-final. 'But we have to prove it over ninety minutes or more.' There was to be more, much more. No, this was not a game that it would be in any way tolerable to lose.

There was another reason to want England to win. Incredibly, they had started to play football that, while not quite Brazilian in its beauty, was not unattractive. Having started with an unsightly performance against Ireland, they had gradually improved in matches against Egypt, Holland, Belgium and Cameroon. England had the better of the luck in the two latter games – a last-minute goal against Belgium and two late penalties against Cameroon – but, galvanised by the bullish grace of Paul Gascoigne, they had probably earned their good fortune. Of Gascoigne, Robson would say after the Germany game: 'He could be on the threshold of something quite unique in the English game.' As it turned out, which is not nearly as well as it should have done, Gascoigne never

quite crossed that threshold, not profession-
ally, not personally. But what he achieved in
Italy changed the English game for good.
Suddenly football seemed much less ugly.
Gazzamania was to follow and English football found a new hero and, in a way, itself. It
also became a modern business. Two days
before the England-West Germany match,
Rupert Murdoch announced that his four-
channel satellite TV service had lost £250
million but predicted that it would soon break
even. Of course, that wasn't to happen until
BSkyB landed the rights to the new
Premiership football in 1992 and there is a
sound argument that says it wouldn't have
happened if Gascoigne hadn't taught the
country how to fall in love again with the
national game.

The Germans, too, had ridden their luck. In
the quarter-final against Czechoslovakia an
Austrian referee named, in a remarkable
coincidence, Helmet Kohl awarded a dubious
penalty against the Czechs and sent one of
their players off in an equally controversial
incident. Foreshadowing what was to come,
the quarter-finals were dominated by
penalties. Aside from the three in the
Germany and England games, the Argentina

versus Yugoslavia match went to penalties following two goalless hours of play in which Yugoslavia were the superior side, despite having a player sent off. The Yugoslav manager refused to watch and dismissed the shoot-out as a 'lottery'. After a mix-up with their running order of penalty-takers between Brnovic and Hadzibegic, who both missed, Yugoslavia lost 2-3. They were an extremely talented side but it was to be the last competition in which they would play together. Within a week, Yugoslavian troops from Serbia had marched into Priština, the capital of a little-heard-of southern province called Kosovo, to put down protests by striking ethnic Albanian workers. Yugoslavia had set out on its long road to self-destruction. It sounds trite to suggest it, but could history have taken a different path if Brnovic and Hadzibegic had scored their penalties?

Diego Maradona was one of two Argentinian players to fail in the shoot-out against Yugoslavia. His explanation was in keeping with his devout appreciation of the game's unforeseen caprices: 'I think God made me miss that penalty for superstitious reasons.' The night before England met West Germany, God was in a less superstitious mood. Argentina managed to draw against Italy in the other semi-final and once again won the penalty shoot-out, with Maradona scoring this time.

How well did England play against West Germany? At the time I recall thinking that it was a magnificent display. Reviewing the tape now I realise that my expectations were not high. Bobby Robson had steered England to the quarter-final stage in the previous World Cup, only to go out to God moving in ridiculous and sublime ways through the body of Maradona. Argentina were the eventual winners. Why then couldn't England make it to the final this time round? What reason did the English have to feel pessimistic? True, the Germans had reached the final of the previous two World Cups, but they were playing no better than England. Yet, writing on the eve of the semi-final, David Lacey of the *Guardian* revealed the enormous underbelly of English doubt. 'Even now, the idea of England playing in the 1990 World Cup final stretches the imagination. After so many years of non-achievement it is difficult to come to terms with the fact that if West Germany are beaten in Turin tonight

A NIGHT TO REMEMBER

Bobby Robson will end his career as England manager on Sunday in a position to emulate Alf Ramsay's triumph of 1966.'

The prospect of victory seemed to discomfit commentators. They were unused to it. Defeat they could handle. They knew that story, knew what they could do with it. But triumph? The most trying problem would be repositioning Robson as a great leader. After the dire draw against the Republic of Ireland, one tabloid had gone so far as to recommend that England under Robson should withdraw from the tournament. The man had withstood such punishment during his eight years as manager, so many verbal punches, that his face began to seem as if it were imploding. The stress had eaten away from the inside, leaving his features at the mercy of events, so that he came, unfortunately, to resemble his *Spitting Image* puppet: a sentimental caricature of unguarded expressions, contorted into shape by external pressures as if cruelly yanked by strings. Now he was standing on the edge of the most irresistible vindication. If fate would only smile on him he would regain face. He might even regain control of it.

Robson's prematch assessment of the West Germany game was not wrong. 'I think', he said, 'it will be a battle of wills.' Much had been made of the fact that, halfway through the tournament, Robson, apparently persuaded by the players, switched from the traditional 4-4-2 formation to the 5-3-2 set-up favoured by many continental sides, which featured a sweeper or *librero*. In the event, for England, it tended to mean three centre-backs. After the game the tactical post-mortem was less sophisticated. The only question that was raised was whether England had practised penalties.

For years it was said that the Germans practised penalties with a methodical determination to banish mistakes. Klinsmann claimed not long ago that this was simply a myth. 'No, no,' he told the BBC, when asked on a penalty special called *On The Spot*, 'we never practised it. I mean, I think it turned out fine for us because in a certain way we were lucky and in another way maybe we were just mentally very strong in that moment. What we always did is left it open to the players. If they wanted to take a couple of penalties after training was over, a few ones did it, a few said "No, if I practise now I'm going to miss it in the game." So it was up to the players.'

He went on to say how in 1990 he was due

to take a penalty but asked not to because he had not played well and did not feel confident. Then, shifting from the first to the third and on to the second person like some unreliable narrator in experimental fiction, Klinsmann attempted to explain the reasons for the Germans' psychological strength. 'Maybe it's also part of our mentality because of the history of Germany. They had to rebuild their country twice. They had to work hard. They were always ambitious. So maybe because of the ambition they have inside of themselves they were also able to cope with the pressure all the time. That's part of your mentality.'

Is Klinsmann telling the truth or is this an example of the fabled German sense of humour? Perhaps it was a case of the former Spurs striker showing his PR skills once again and playing to his beloved English media, making it all up to enable us to feel less incompetent. Or he may have been instructed by the German FA to say as much in an effort, in psychiatric language, to fuck with our minds. In the wake of 1990, there is no doubt that everyone was so convinced that the Germans had practised penalties that, presumably fearing yet more obloquy, Robson began implying that England also had practised penalties. A decade on and Robson seems to have persuaded himself that this was the case. He told me that the preparations had been meticulous – talking, practising, selecting – while emphasising, as you must, that no training-ground exercise can simulate the live, pressured experience.

Chris Waddle has said that England did not practise penalties, although Lineker practised them because it was part of his job. 'In '90,' stated Waddle unambiguously on *On The Spot*, which he co-presented with Lineker, 'we never practised.' Waddle and Robson can't both be right. David Platt, treading with the diplomatic care of a man who is now a manager himself, told me that he couldn't remember if England practised penalties.

The question of practice is one to which I shall come back as, indeed, would English football intermittently over the next ten years. In passing, though, I'll mention now that I have never understood the line of argument which says there is no point in practising because it's completely different on the day. Can you imagine Tiger Woods or Nick Faldo not bothering with four- or five-foot putts on the practice green because there is no pressure involved? If you aim for the inside of the side netting with a shot that is reasonably well struck, you will always score. What's wrong with getting to know where that side netting is?

But all that nearly didn't matter. Nearly. Is there a more saddening word in sport? England opened brightly, confidently; they were all movement and space and shape for the first twenty minutes, and no little flair. Gascoigne imposed himself on Lothar Matthaeus, perhaps then the best midfield player in Europe. Mark Wright had Klinsmann in his pocket and, with Gascoigne's encouragement, Chris Waddle was beginning to look like the player he could be: deft, quick, dangerous. He was beating his marker. In the thirty-fourth minute, a ball broke loose in the centre circle and Waddle turned and hit it with the glorious abandon of a man with destiny on his side. The ball left his foot as if it knew where it was headed – over the goalkeeper and into the net – even from so far away. You could have called it a chip had it not been struck with such assured power. Somehow the German keeper, Illgner, arched miraculously backwards and channelled enough strength into his fingertips to redirect the ball on to the crossbar. The action took place in a second and in that same second the referee blew his whistle for a debatable infringement by England. It wouldn't have counted, but it already had. England had shown that they were capable of the unexpected. And even they themselves had not been sure of that.

Even so it was the Germans who emerged the stronger after half-time. On the hour they scored from a hugely deflected free kick. There was a crushing needlessness about the goal, a bent logic, that not for the last time reaffirmed my atheism. I also wondered if at forty, on his 124th cap, Peter Shilton was too old to be playing at this level. England took control for the remainder of normal time. Pearce nearly scored with a header, then Waddle was denied a certain penalty. Just as there is an art to scoring penalties, there is also an art, a dark art, to winning them. Waddle never mastered either. I saw him have numerous appeals turned down when he played for Tottenham. The problem was that with his heavy-footed, sloping gait and hang-dog demeanour he looked much slower than he actually was. This meant that defenders were fooled into thinking they could get the ball. Unfortunately, referees were equally duped and failed to see that Waddle had more often than not pushed the ball on before being clobbered.

England had reverted to their familiar 4-4-2 shape when Lineker equalised. It felt like coming up from the depths, like gulping fresh air, like justice. Although not a typical Lineker goal – it was too far out and left-footed – there were familiar characteristics: inelegance, speed and uncanny precision. England were about to play their third 120-minute game in the space of eight days. Not that you could tell. In the first half of extra time, they performed better than they had done in the whole game, perhaps for many years. Waddle hit the inside of the post with a goalbound shot – his third piece of bad luck, including the crossbar incident and the unawarded penalty, but not his last. Gascoigne was flying, high on adrenalin and his own ability. He beat two Germans then launched himself at the ball as it ran away to a third. He missed. Berthold went down and rolled over three times with Brechtian theatricality – not only was he acting, he appeared to want to show us he was acting. The referee, Jose Ramiz Wright from Brazil, did not seem to recognise the

German's dramatic reference, his agit-prop attempt to knock down the fourth wall, and instead booked the Englishman, thereby excluding him from a place in the final. Gascoigne, 'the priapic monolith in the Mediterranean sun', as Karl Miller called him, began to cry. You could see that those tears had an immediate iconographic appeal but no one could have known that they would wash away the decade's worth of grit and grime under which English football had become buried.

In the second half Buchwald hit the post for Germany and Platt had a headed goal disallowed for offside. No one complained but in fact Platt and his fellow English players were onside when Waddle took a free kick from the right, even by the old ruling in which the attacker had to be behind the defender. Such incidents don't show up in the record books and, in time, they even fade from memory, but on these details history is made or unmade. The irony of this encounter was that the two northern European sides had provided the most Italian occasion of the Italia '90, which is to say the most overwrought, the most emotional, the most operatic. With the conclusion of extra time, however, events turned Greek, they went *epic*.

England had never taken part in a penalty shoot-out before. This was unknown territory. Even John Motson seemed unprepared. 'If somebody had said to me at the start of the World Cup,' said Motson, ' "Well, you'll be commentating on a penalty shoot-out to decide whether or not England play in the final," I must admit, I would have swallowed very hard indeed.'

Out in the centre circle, where the two teams, managers, subs and physios were gathered, there was much hard swallowing of oxygen and liquid and words. No one had much to say. They patted one another on the back, but they were locked inside their own thoughts, mourners at their own funerals. Robson, wearing a light grey suit and a smiling grimace, consoled Gascoigne, who was on his knees. Franz Beckenbauer, the German coach, walked around looking like Art Garfunkel in *Bad Timing*: the imperious shrink who remains above weak emotions. He seemed unruffled and supremely confident. Shilton won the toss, which meant that England would start. If you win, you have no choice. The England players nominated to be the first five stood solemnly with their hands behind their backs. The rest sat down, or rather collapsed down. The waiting seemed to go on for ages. Checking the running order of penalty-takers couldn't take that long. It was as if the players were given time to consider the enormity of what it meant. But time was the last thing they wanted.

Lineker, who had already scored two penalties in the previous round, was eventually the first to go. At thirty, he still looked the baby-faced assassin. Nothing about him appeared intimidating, except his goal-scoring record. He did nothing fancy. He put the ball down, pulled up his left sock, walked calmly back, ran up and hit the ball hard and low to the goalkeeper's right. Illgner went left. He trotted back and Waddle shook his hand. Brehme followed and hit practically the same shot, but even better – harder, further to the right, it hit the inside of the side netting. Shilton dived the right way but there was no way he could save it.

Bob Wilson told me that a yard inside each post was to all intents and purposes out of the reach of goalkeepers. He thought that they should concentrate on saving within the other six yards. The lesson for the penalty-taker, therefore, is to hit the ball at that yard either side of the central six yards. Beardsley, who was England's second penalty-taker, didn't quite get his shot inside one of those yards. His delivery was totally undisguised. Everything about his body shape and run-up suggested that he was aiming for the upper right side of the goal, to the goalkeeper's left. If a right-footed player approaches the ball from his left, then usually his intention is to put it to the right (the keeper's left). Beardsley turned his body so that his left side was facing the goalkeeper and struck the ball low with the side of his right foot. There was only one area the ball could be heading and Illgner went for it. The ball was too high, though, and Illgner's despairing right hand was a foot away at least. He had gone early, but not as early as he needed to – or would do. He had also prematurely stepped off his line, thereby narrowing the angle.

By contrast Shilton waited on each penalty till the last microsecond before he committed himself. This meant that each time he went the correct way. But could he have saved one or more if he had gone earlier? A number of footballers, in particular Mark Crossley, the Middlesborough goalkeeper and one of the finest penalty-savers in the business, told me that they thought Shilton played safe. 'I was disappointed with him,' said Crossley. 'You have to take a chance at that level. And he didn't.' Matthaeus was up next. He, too, had scored a penalty in the previous round. Matthaeus had a powerful shot and he aimed it to Shilton's right. Like Beardsley's, however, it was a telegraphed kick. In slow motion you can see that Shilton bounced at the point at which he instinctively knew that Matthaeus was committed to follow through with his intended kick. But Shilton didn't dive. He waited, and went on the next beat. He missed the ball by no more than two inches. He looked angry – with himself or Matthaeus it was impossible to know – and took a few seconds to pick himself up. The received wisdom at the time was that all the German penalties were unsavable. This is not so. A spectacular dive by Shilton is what would have been required to stop Matthaeus; spectacular but not impossible. In the final, when the Germans were awarded a penalty, it was Brehme, not Matthaeus, who stepped up. Perhaps Matthaeus was spooked by his close shave.

Platt arrived at the spot. First his head and torso and then, a short while later, his legs and, finally, his bottom. His was an unlikely posture, with his comically puffed-out chest, as if it were permanently primed for one of his late runs and salmon leaps. But Platt was one of the unpredicted stars of the tournament. He'd come into the side when John Barnes was injured and his goal in the last minute of extra time against Belgium had confirmed his value as a deep-lying marksman. A fastidious character, he had, he told me, already decided the night before which side to place the penalty if he took one. 'But I noticed that the keeper had dived left for both Lineker and Beardsley so I changed my mind and decided to go for his right.'

He hit the ball to Illgner's right but the keeper anticipated as much and was a yard off his line and going right when Platt's boot made contact. Although Illgner got his fingers to the ball, all he could do was deflect it into the goal. Platt said his 'heart skipped a beat'. He turned and beamed one of those relieved grins that he couldn't have stopped even if he wanted to. Illgner said after the match that because he'd touched the Platt shot he 'knew' that he would save the next one.

Karlheinz Riedle allowed Shilton no chance with his penalty. Again the goalkeeper went the right way, but the ball was too high and too far to his left. Three-all. Back in Archway I was now speaking exclusively in expletives. Then Pearce strolled up. In those shorts. Who could say what kind of pain he was in? He certainly didn't look happy. But then he never did. He looked committed. He looked so committed that he looked as though he should have been committed. Psycho: fearless and fearsome. The man, as they say in Spanish, had *cojones*, even if he had allowed them such precious little space.

In Robson's view, Pearce was England's best penalty-taker, better even than Lineker, the regular taker. He thought that the fourth penalty was possibly the most vital. He was right, although not in the way he had hoped. Pearce had power and precision. You felt that even if a keeper got his hand to a strike from Pearce it would probably fold at the wrist. Illgner didn't get his hand to the ball. Pearce ran up fairly straight and drove the ball with remarkable force. Perhaps he had noticed that Illgner was diving early or perhaps he just let rip. The ball went screaming two feet off the ground towards the centre of the goal. Possibly because the left-footed Pearce was that much more difficult to read, Illgner fractionally delayed his dive before leaping to his right. He still got it wrong but it meant that his legs were air-bound at the right height to connect with the ball, which they did and without folding. It just happened. Nearly. Nearly. Oh, so nearly.

Some knowledge is too painful to accept all at once. You need to receive it in instalments. I knew on some intuitive level, as everyone did, that England were out right then. All of a sudden I was aware that I was watching television, that these events were taking place hundreds of miles away. A cruel distance appeared between me and the images on the box. Too cruel. I was in no mood to deal with reality. Not yet. That could, and would, come later. So, for the moment, I slipped into self-preserving denial. Had I been Pearce, I think I would have collected the ball as it bounced off Illgner, kicked it into the net, and explained to the referee that it was in fact a goal. I would have lost all dignity. Pearce just turned and walked back, his head slightly bowed, his face impassive yet transparently sad.

The next stage of denial was to hope that Shilton would save from Thon, the fourth German penalty-taker. Shilton had three rules that he followed in penalty situations (why does everyone have three rules with penalties?), which he outlined in his 1988 book, *Goalkeeping in Action*:

(1) Try to dictate the terms.
(2) Stand up as long as you can.
(3) Read the kicker's run-up.

After more than two hours of wonderfully competitive football, no one had the appetite for gamesmanship, so the first rule did not properly apply. He did stand up for as long as he could. And that's why he was able to read the kicker's run-up so successfully. Shilton had tremendous confidence in his reflexes. With his compact frame and unnaturally long arms – the result, it is said, of hanging from door frames as a child – he always had a wild simian quality about him, as if he was ready to spring at anything that moved. With Thon, however, he didn't read the run-up until too late. He leaned as if to go to his right but then adjusted to dive left. Some goalkeepers, of course, feign to go one way while always meaning to go the other. I don't think this was Shilton's plan. His weight was on the wrong foot. Thon's shot, to Shilton's left, was not a cert. It was probably the poorest of Germany's four. Shilton missed it by inches. Incredible, really, that he had managed to get so close after seeming first to move to his right. If Shilton had saved any of his penalties, even the strictest referee – and there is no such thing with penalties – would not have ordered them to be retaken. And that, I would say, is why he would never have saved them. Goalkeeping is mostly about percentages, but with penalties a little gambling is also required. The idea of not going before the shot only made sense if the penalties were not well taken. The Germans had not given anyone reason to believe that their penalties would be anything less than proficient. They went for the corners and, as Waddle put it, all their shots were 'laces' – hit with the front of the foot.

Paul Gascoigne was due to take the fifth penalty but, still reeling from the booking that ruled him out of the final, he asked to be removed from the list. So Waddle took his place. Waddle, I think, was man of the match. He had hit the crossbar with one of the finest shots of any World Cup, he had been denied a clear-cut penalty and he had hit the inside of the post in extra time. He had scored down the years, and would continue to score, some fabulous free kicks from twenty-five yards or more with a defensive wall situated in the way. But from twelve yards with just a goalkeeper? Well, he wasn't a penalty-taker.

Originally he intended to place the shot. With Pearce having missed, however, he went for power. 'I thought, if he does get anything on it . . . it will still go in,' he later explained. I had tried to get Waddle to talk about the penalty but, understandably, he was very reluctant. Here was one of the most gifted players England had produced in my lifetime and he would be remembered for his lifetime for what happened with that penalty. He told me that he was fed up answering the same questions and said that I should fax him mine and he'd think about it. I did so and then rewatched what he had to say on the matter in *On The Spot*. 'People have said to me,' Waddle said, baffled, '"When you put the ball on the penalty spot, what went through your head?" When I think about it now, it was obviously "Hit the target." They say, "What was going on about you?" I never thought about anything.'

What had I asked Waddle in my fax? 'What were you thinking about?' was one question, while another was, 'Can you recall anything that was going on about you?' Needless to say, he never got back.

Dennis Lillee in his prime took shorter run-ups than Waddle with that fifth penalty. To everyone watching it was sorely apparent that the target was in no danger. But Waddle wasn't watching, he was *doing*, and only he could know how things seemed to him. His execution was not dissimilar to his preparation insofar as they were both over the top. The ball skewed off his boot like a snooker ball off a drunk's cue. Pearce was crouching with a blue towel around his shoulders in the centre circle, looking like a boxer waiting for a decision that he knew would go against him. Illgner was nowhere near the ball but, unhappily, the ball was nowhere near the goal. It passed over the right-hand corner of the German's crossbar and kept going, and going, and with it went the dream that England had hardly dared begin to dream. The ball was no doubt retrieved later that night, perhaps somewhere on the outskirts of the city, but it took six years for England to come within sight of the fantasy again.

CHAPTER THREE

Psycho Drama

At Italia '90, the players who lined up against Illgner had only to deal with the pressure of what was unfolding at that present time, which, it should be acknowledged, was close to intolerable. At Euro '96 the England players who took part in two penalty shoot-outs had an additional pressure to contend with: what had happened in the past. Only David Platt, Stuart Pearce and Paul Gascoigne survived in the team that played six years on, and Gascoigne had not participated in the original penalty kicks. Still, the knowledge of that previous failure was carried by all the players, and spectators, into the quarter-final shoot-out against Spain. The result of that contest, and also one particular incident within it, changed England's perception of the penalty decider. In the six years that followed Bobby Robson's side's narrow defeat, penalties, if they were mentioned at all, tended to be dismissed with words like 'luck' and 'lottery'. With England winning now, and particularly after they had been outplayed by Spain, that view was to undergo some revision. Phrases such as 'will-power' and 'mental strength' quickly gained a much wider currency. That England had triumphed was seen as a testament of the team's character. And the personification of this indomitable spirit was Stuart 'Psycho' Pearce.

Pearce was, and is, not the sort of player to publicise his inner thoughts. A man of few words, who rarely gives interviews, he left the impression that he didn't have any inner thoughts to publicise. Indeed, you could imagine that to him the whole idea of inner thinking was worryingly effete. He had barely ever referred to what happened in Turin, save in the most cursory fashion. So nobody knew what to expect when he stepped up to take the third penalty for England. That's not to say that there wasn't a tremendous sense of apprehension. My first thought when I realised that he was one of the chosen five penalty-takers was *what's he doing?* I was more than a little surprised, in spite of Pearce's granite reputation, to see him putting himself through the ordeal again. Terry Venables admitted afterwards that he himself had been thinking of not selecting Pearce for penalty duty. 'But it was stupid of me really,' he said. 'He came straight up to me and asked to take one.' My second thought was relief that his shorts now provided for movement.

Much of the appeal of the penalty shoot-out, it's reasonable to say, lies in its macabre nature. Just as we watch Formula One racing secretly awaiting a crash, so do we watch a shoot-out in craven anticipation of the miss – the sudden extinction of all hope. Ghoulishness, however, is only half the story. An equally compelling aspect of the shoot-out is the strange psychological terrain, filled with isolation, that it inhabits. If, as the old adage says, you are never more alone than in a crowd, then it must get mighty lonesome around that penalty spot. Out there the taker is supported by the trust of his teammates, the hopes of his fans and, at the highest level, the dreams of his countrymen. Thousands of people are present and millions, perhaps hundreds of millions, may be watching on television. Yet down that mean street that runs from centre circle to the twelve-yard spot a good man must walk on his own. Pearce was prepared to walk the walk.

But what if he missed again? How could he bear it? How could *I* bear it?

Euro '96 had begun, from an English angle, in typical style. The press were united in their contempt for the England team and their chances in the competition. Photographs of some of the players drinking on a pre-tournament tour in the Far East had deeply offended the nation's sportswriters, whose strict code of temperance has long provided a model of unbending asceticism. A kerfuffle, involving a broken TV set, on the aeroplane returning to London only underlined the media's view that the England players were a group of debauched no-hopers. Venables cordoned off the team with a binding phrase – 'collective responsibility' – designed to protect individuals from specific blame. Then came a dull draw against Switzerland in the opening game and the press launched a barrage of insults. The *Daily Mirror* said England were 'the laughing stock of the world'. The *Sun* suggested that 'The only thing we'll win is the *Men Behaving Badly* trophy for drunken also-rans'. (As in 1990, England went on to win the good behaviour, or fair play, award.)

Not for the first time, this ill-feeling was not shared by the fans or the public. People were just pleased that Graham Taylor, the disciple of Charles Hughes's regressive football, was no longer in charge of England. The release of a record, 'Three Lions', had given the crowd something to sing and a sense of optimism, an 'Englishness' that wasn't xenophobic, a nationalism that was humorous and non-confrontational. For once there was a feeling of unity at Wembley. Nevertheless a couple of corners remained to be turned before this hope was to become confident expectation. And those corners, as David Coleman might have said, were penalties.

In England's second game they were leading 1-0 when Scotland were awarded a spot kick, which was taken by Gary McAllister. Just before McAllister was about to strike it, the ball moved off the penalty spot, a result, perhaps, of some bizarre micro-weather system spontaneously generated by the tension within the stadium. It was a small but not insignificant movement. 'David Seaman still can't understand why McAllister didn't stop,' Bob Wilson told me. 'He said McAllister saw the ball on the move. Yet he still he carried on with it.'

PSYCHO DRAMA

'The funny thing was,' said McAllister afterwards, 'I had decided to hit the ball straight and a little off the ground, because goalkeepers usually move early. If I had side-footed it for the corner, he would have dropped his cap on it. Given the stage of the game I felt I had to score. I simply didn't hit it quite straight enough.'

Perhaps the moving ball affected his aim. If so, why did he run the risk? Why didn't he return the ball to the spot, as he had every right to do? Was he too anxious to get the thing done? McAllister spoke of his state of mind before the penalty. 'I had no qualms about taking the kick. I've been doing it for teams as far back as I can remember. *And I didn't feel the weight of the occasion*, either. I just took it automatically, as I would any other set piece, like a free kick or a corner kick.'

The italics are mine. Plainly, in his own mind, McAllister did not feel particularly pressurised. Or he didn't think he felt pres-surised. Or he didn't want to say he did. As we know, Seaman stopped the ball with his elbow. The game moved swiftly to the other end and Gascoigne scored a magnificent self-created goal. The Scots fans never forgave McAllister. He was out of football for a period afterwards with an injury but when he returned the reception the crowd gave him was so hostile that he announced his retirement as an international player.

In the following game, Alan Shearer showed what a converted penalty can do. Breaking the deadlock against Holland, it led to a four-goal rout in what was, without doubt, England's finest performance since winning the World Cup in 1966. The tabloids apologised or backtracked, the England players were heroes to a man, 'Three Lions', with its persuasive refrain – 'It's coming home . . . Football's coming home' – was the soundtrack of the summer, and across a nation, England, that was officially allowed to celebrate itself only in times of war or royal weddings, a kind of latent hysteria broke out.

This was the heightened reality – the right hereness, right nowness – in which Pearce took his penalty. As he walked back to begin his run-up, his face was a rictus of deathly concentration. The Spanish goalkeeper, Zubizarreta had gone the correct way for the previous two kicks, although he failed to save them. Just before Pearce let fly, the Spaniard dived, again correctly, to his left. But Pearce hit the ball with pace and too far into the corner to reach. Goal. Pearce turned to his right, staring for a moment into the open spaces of his release, and then threw a wild punch into the air. Walking towards the crowd, screaming, 'Come on! Come on!' he unleashed another punch and stopped. That's when something monstrous and repressed was exorcised. Thrusting his jaw forwards, his lower lip folded down, Pearce let out a bloodthirsty scream. Richard Williams, writing in the *Guardian*, was reminded of 'a Ralph Steadman cartoon of a football hooligan'. Clearly, you would not have wanted to spill your drink on Pearce just then. This was like a terrifying cameo of psychosis. But it was equally apparent that such a supremely visceral scene had deeper origins than Pearce's unnatural aggression, which, after all, he had never made a point of hiding. It was if his id had escaped.

'It's strange really,' Pearce himself observed. 'It's nothing I pre-planned, thinking to myself, if I score I'm going to go stupid, or whatever. I'm not a big emotional man, possibly. But maybe there was something underlying there that said, hang on a minute: Get in!'

Don't you find that 'possibly' unutterably

moving? Pearce was wrong, though. His improvised haka did not say 'Get in!' Hang on a minute, it was all about: Get out! Out vile memory. Out! On the way back, he passed Seaman, whom he encouraged to try even harder: 'Now fuckin' save it!'

The moral of the psychodrama, if it hadn't already been gleaned, was that penalties had a lot to do with psychology. Graham Taylor once remarked that 'footballers are no different from human beings'. A controversial idea, perhaps, but not without its merits. In matters psychological, however, human beings are notoriously difficult to pin down, and footballers even more so. Take, for example, the question of penalties and pressure. All footballers say that taking a penalty in training is not the same as taking one in front of 75,000 spectators. The other thing they say is that they don't notice the spectators. With a crowd present, they agree, there is much more tension and expectation. But they also say they don't feel the tension and expectation. McAllister said as much. David Platt told me that it was difficult for fans to understand but footballers are often so focused that they don't fully realise what the outcome of a game can mean to people who are not actually playing in it. 'It's not until a few days later', he explained, 'that it sinks in and you realise the significance of what's happened.' Chris Waddle, who has had much less to savour with his penalty experiences, confirms this sense of detachment. 'You're probably the only one who's not really thinking about the result,' he said. Gareth Southgate was even more emphatic: 'I think football doesn't have the same importance to me, ironically, as to people who watch it.'

I suspect some of this is post-rationalisation. I also think that just because a footballer is not quaking with nerves does not mean that he is not experiencing pressure. He may be able to block out the external causes of tension – the noise, the crowd – but it can still have an impact on the unconscious mind, if such a thing exists. Let's assume that it does, for a moment. Even the most unreconstructed Freudian would accept that there is no map of the unconscious. By the same token, someone like myself, who is sceptical about the claims of the psychological sciences, is prepared to concede that people offer signs to their behaviour of which they may not be consciously aware. The trick with penalties, presumably, is to identify those signs which suggest a player is likely to be adversely affected by the mental strain of taking a penalty before he is an a position to take one.

A psychologist named George Sik, and his colleague Stephen Smith, spent some time in the early nineties applying personality profile techniques, of the kind commonly used in business recruitment, to the world of football. He issued questionnaires to fifty-five footballers from Crystal Palace, Sheffield United and Celtic. The answers he received back suggested that players had enormously differing responses to stressful situations. When Dr Sik (pronounced, you may be relieved to hear, 'Shick') gave his findings to the British Psychological Society in 1992, he warned that managers seemed to take little account of their players' psychological predisposition, and cited penalty shoot-outs as an example where this neglect could prove costly. At the time, Sik's conclusions went largely unheard outside the profession of occupational psychology.

Four years later, one of the players that Dr Sik had profiled was to miss a vital penalty. A while later, Dr Sik spoke of the unfortunate man, without actually naming him, to a meeting of the British Association for the Advancement of Science. 'There were a number of characteristics that would have led anybody trained in the field to spot that he was not the best choice for the job [of penalty-taking],' explained Dr Sik. He found that the player 'will volunteer for difficult tasks but, at the same time, he is cautious, likes to plan things in advance, and is pessimistic about outcomes, highly strung and nervous about big occasions'.

By the sound of it, you wouldn't let the guy *watch* a penalty, never mind take one. Not, then, the most flattering of character assessments. At least, that's how the player himself saw it. Dr Sik's paper gained widespread coverage this time round. Although theoretically anonymous, the number of potential suspects to which he might be referring was obviously less than two. Perhaps understandably, the nervous pessimist complained. He has since taken two penalties, one of them the decider in another penalty shoot-out. And missed both.

Penalty-taking, Dr Sik informed me, is a game within a game. Although it demands similar skills to those used in open play, the penalty requires a different mindset. 'There are players', he said, 'whose personalities are fundamentally unsuited to it.' He argues that there are two types of penalty misses. One is random and has nothing to do with a player's outlook or mental approach. It's just that even the best penalty-takers will miss at some point. He cites Pearce's penalty in 1990 as an instance. The other is almost guaranteed because the player has the wrong psychological profile. 'Some players will simply always miss penalties.'

In a piece he wrote for the *New Yorker*, the journalist Malcolm Gladwell examined the meaning of the terms 'choking' and 'panicking', which are often used to describe a sportsperson's sudden and dramatic loss of ability. In fact, while these words are frequently referred to as if they were interchangeable, there is a crucial distinction between them. Essentially it's this: professionals choke and amateurs panic. Given the right circumstances, anyone can panic; whereas to choke properly you need years of experience.

If called upon to perform a new physical task, we rely on explicit learning. Which is to say, we consciously think about what we are doing. For the weekend golfer or occasional visitor to a snooker hall, it is unlikely that the task of striking a golf ball or potting a black will ever become second nature. You'll still address the tee in an awkwardly deliberate manner, still feel as if the cue is not so much an extension of your arm as someone else's leg. But when an athlete practises a manoeuvre over and over, the information is stored as 'implicit learning' in an area of the brain called the basal ganglia. This is the process that transforms years of repetitive actions into unconscious execution. Recent research suggests that top ball players may not even look at balls when they hit them, at least not with their eyes. Some scientists think that implicit learning enables athletes instinctively to 'see' without having to focus on the object they are aiming to hit. If that is true, then the old saw about always keeping your eye on the ball is in need of urgent revision.

In stress situations, though, even the most seasoned professionals can revert to explicit learning. In other words, they start thinking about keeping their eyes on the ball. Gladwell cited as two textbook examples of choking, Jana Novotna's collapse against Steffi Graf in the 1993 Wimbledon final and Greg Norman's inexplicable disintegration in the final round of the 1996 Masters, allowing Nick Faldo to win. In both cases top-flight pros started playing like amateurs. They returned to first principles and started thinking. And thinking is something you don't want to find yourself doing when you're competing in the upper reaches of sport.

Panicking, by contrast, is what you do when you have nothing else to refer to. Both implicit and explicit learning go out the window and all that is left is animal fear. Your mind goes blank and there is not enough stored information, not enough practice, to enable even basic function. It's what happens, say, to inexperienced divers when they momentarily lose their oxygen supply. Gladwell speculates that this is what happened to John F Kennedy Jnr when he crashed his light aircraft. Panicking, then, is very different to choking. But the extraordinary thing about the England players is that when it comes to penalties, they have choked *and* panicked. Some of them have simply not had the experience to choke, having never before taken a penalty, so they must have panicked.

I wondered why footballers – Waddle was just one example – invariably said that they were not aware of what was going on around them before they took a penalty. 'It's the mammalian response to stress,' said Dr Sik. You close down or block out surrounding things. But we're a little bit too clever for our own good. We still know that the situation is different. We can feel the adrenalin-rush. One thing that sports psychologists agree on is, the best way to prepare is to try and make the adrenalin work for you. Try and be positive.'

David Platt, who was the kind of self-improver as a player who would probably have owned books and videos on sports psychology and personal development, said something remarkably similar. 'I tried to shut everything out, take all the emotion away. I tried to use the pressure as motivation. I wanted the responsibility.'

But then some players say they want the responsibility because they feel responsible. They think that is what is expected of them. How can a manager know which is the genuine article? Dr Sik says that a proper diagnostic personality questionnaire would help do the trick. In reality, managers tend to rely on their own instincts about their charges. Besides, such are their own weighty responsibilities and pressures, they often don't get round to learning what a given foot-baller's penalty-scoring record might be, much less spend time analysing the meaning of their players' innermost conflicts. Who'd be a manager?

Not all players disguise their true feelings. Some make them perfectly obvious even to the untrained eye. When Paul Ince sat in the centre circle in the Euro '96 semi-final against Germany and looked in the opposite direction to the shoot-out taking place, a doctorate in psychology was not needed to work out that he did not relish the prospect of taking part. Once again England had played an enthral-ling game of football against their greatest rivals, in which they showed neat skills and stirring passion. Once again a lithe English winger – Anderton, this time, not Waddle – hit the post in extra time. Had he scored England would have won because a new system of the so-called 'Golden Goal' was operating, which meant the first goal scored in extra time would be the winner. Once again Gascoigne mistimed a fateful slide – missing the ball at an open goal by inches, on this occasion, rather than hitting a German avant-garde thespian. Once again the score was 1-1.

PSYCHO DRAMA

History was about to repeat itself: the first time as tragedy, the second time as tragedy.

You could sympathise with Ince's position, one that faced away from the action, because the alternative, the one that faced towards it, was about as comfortable as watching a loved one undergo open-heart surgery. Des Lynam felt moved to apologise to television viewers and said that he would understand if they viewed the shoot-out from behind the sofa. In fact, it might be argued that Ince showed commendable responsibility in turning his back on the responsibility of the shoot-out. I know I was relieved. I had always been impressed, if that's the right word, by Ince's unerring ability to find the goalkeeper from any distance. With most players, if the ball bounces in front of them thirty yards from the goal, it's a safe bet that they will volley it into the stands. Not Ince. Few footballers can strike a ball more cleanly or more accurately. He is unfailingly on target. Always at the goal, and always at the goalie in the goal. I don't know if Ince possesses a subconscious desire to let the keeper know how hard he strikes the ball and, at that moment, I didn't care. All I knew was that it's not a talent one needs to see demonstrated in a shoot-out.

Others didn't see it that way. Many observers pointed out Ince's self-built cult of the 'Guv'nor'. They argued that a man who awarded himself such a commanding sobriquet should not have been looking at an empty goal at the wrong end of the pitch. Platt had said to me that he had one overriding reason for wanting to take a penalty: 'Because I believe that I am a leader.' If Ince was a leader, said his critics, his job was to inspire his teammates and volunteer for action.

Once more England went first. Shearer, reassuringly, was number one on the list. Everything about Shearer at that time said goal. He'd had a superb tournament, although he had come into it on the back of a prolonged goal famine. He had scored England's goal with a header some two hours before, just two minutes after the teams had kicked off. He was confident and physically imposing. He made the goalkeeper seem like a token presence and, I suspect, that's how the goalkeeper felt, too. Shearer's kick was viciously disguised. His body seemed poised to swing towards the keeper's right, which is the way Kopke went. But the instant before he struck the ball, Shearer opened his foot and placed it, with power, high in the other corner.

PSYCHO DRAMA

Hassler's reply was the complete opposite but no more stoppable. Low and to Seaman's left, it bore the mark of a practised touch. If penalty practise really was an optional subject in the Germans' training, Hassler, I feel sure, had been conscientiously revising. There was no doubt that the English camp had been practising. Platt, among a number of other players, confirms that they did. Having lost a European Cup final on penalties when he was Barcelona coach, Venables must have been keenly aware of their importance. The quarter-final against Spain reminded everyone of the likelihood of penalties, as did the other semi-final the previous day in which the Czech Republic defeated France in a shoot-out.

Venables would later say that penalties had 'nothing to do with technique', but I don't think he really believed that. He was protecting his players or, rather, player. He was also talking about the need to be in the right frame of mind. 'A lot of it is psychology,' he told me. Venables is smart enough to know that the two are inextricably entwined. The penalty may be a game that's played in the mind but it's a skill practised with the foot.

Bobby Robson said that a player can

practise too much, and Venables said the same thing. Again, I can't conceive of a golfer saying this about his putting. All right, after two or three hours, a golfer would reluctantly take a break. Robson thought that two or three penalties was enough. Not in a session. But in total. Doubtless he was covering for his own revisionist history of 1990, but his attitude is not uncommon in football. Venables thought more practice was needed. 'But', he told me, 'I wouldn't do it just prior to the game.' Waddle, in conversation with Southgate, suggested that 'ten penalties a day wasn't going to kill anybody'.

Southgate couldn't see players going along with that kind of regime. 'If players are going to stay behind [after a training session], they're more likely to work on another weakness in their game they are more likely to use week in week out. That's just the nature of the job. It is leaving things to chance a little bit but I really don't think players want to spend that time [on taking penalties] . . . I can't really practise things all day that you are only going to do once or twice in your career.'

It would demand no more than five minutes to take ten penalties. During a tournament in which shoot-outs are almost certain to play a role, this seems to me a small but valuable amount of time to devote to something that may well prove excruciatingly decisive. Still, football training sessions are something of a mystery to me. I've watched a few and they have all seemed to be both repetitive and slap-dash, which is an odd combination. Given that it is a team sport, football practice will never have the rigour of, say, tennis practice. The emphasis in football is on organisation rather than skill. Yet I don't get it when managers complain, as they do periodically, about the lack of skilful players around. Some go so far as to ask why it is that so many footballers don't seem able to perform basic skills like trapping the ball. When I hear this I tend to think that if a player has been through a club's training scheme from before his teenage apprenticeship up until first-team football then the blame for his deficiencies must lie partly with the club's training scheme, for which the manager has responsibility. David Platt knows all about that responsibility now – at the time of writing – that he is manager of Nottingham Forest. Four years ago it was the responsibility of the penalty that he took on once more. He said that he had learned from 1990, when he had changed his mind and the keeper got a hand to his shot. This time he was always going to put it to Kopke's left. Again, it wasn't a textbook penalty, because it wasn't quite close enough to the post. However, it was high enough to elude the keeper, who did dive left. With both penalties so far, Kopke had stepped off his line before the ball was kicked. The rule had not yet changed, so in fact he wasn't supposed to move his feet at all. But even today, according to the current law, he would not be allowed to come off his line. No one, not the referee in the penalty box, nor his assistant who was standing on the line just to the side of the goal, said anything to him.

Seaman was also moving before the ball, but not really off his line. A huge man, he was making the most of his physique, standing up tall as long as he could – although not as long as Shilton had. According to Bob Wilson, Seaman has always fancied his chances at reading which way the penalty-taker is going to put the ball. This is the only area of goalkeeping theory on which the player and coach differ. Wilson thinks that a keeper should concentrate on protecting the central six yards of the goal, and accept that he cannot

stop a well-aimed shot. Seaman doesn't like
the idea of that limitation. His approach
involves going fractionally early, although
just after it is too late for the kicker to change
his mind.

The technique didn't work with Strunz,
who slammed the ball into the top right-hand
corner of Seaman's net, while the keeper went
to his left. But it almost worked with Reuter.
In between, Pearce once more proved that
1990 was an aberration. With his right arm
coming up to point to the keeper's left, he hit
the ball low and hard to Kopke's right, sending him the wrong way. My relief at seeing
the ball go in was instantly supplanted by a
stricken anxiety. What would he do now? His
celebration turned out to be sensibly muted,
just a thumb stuck out in a disarmingly Cliff
Richard-like gesture of satisfaction. However,
his facial expression was still not one that
you'd be delighted to see on a dimly-lit street
come nightfall.

Something about Reuter announced a
certain iffiness. People often like to say that
they can tell when a player is going to miss a
penalty, and they most often like to say it after
the penalty has been missed. With Reuter,
though, there was a palpable aura of vinc-

ibility, an inappropriateness of movement, as if he could not suppress his own doubts. Seamen looked dauntingly large. A.S. Byatt, writing for the *Observer*, called him a 'striding scarlet lord, entirely comfortable in his beauty. A bullfighter.' Or a ballfighter. Reuter's run was straight, and therefore slightly ambiguous. He couldn't maintain it. Too eager to get the job over, he opened his body prematurely and signalled his direction. Seaman was off, diving to his left. The ball and the keeper seemed ordained to meet, and they so nearly did. To watch a penalty on video in slow motion is to see the hidden story, the subliminal narrative that leaves only the most fleeting impression on the retina. It is said that instinctive sportsmen, like F1 racing drivers and opening batsmen, see the world slowed down. Goalkeepers, too, you feel, must sometimes apprehend action in a kind of gradualised form. As Seaman lurched across the goal, his arms stretched out to interrupt the flight of Reuter's shot. But just as he fully extended them, Seaman realised that the ball was heading higher. He pushed up his right arm in response and the ball flew an inch over his fingers as his hand was still going up. It was so close that it looked as if he had touched the ball. All of that happened inside the space of 400 milliseconds. Seaman still punched the turf in frustration. It was some way from being a bad penalty, but it was the worst the Germans would offer. And Seaman probably knew that.

The best penalty of the night and of many other nights was Gascoigne's. Not only did he send the keeper the wrong way, he also hit the inside of the side netting. You'd think that with all his nervous tics and uncontrollable energy, Gascoigne would come apart at the penalty spot. In fact, the reverse happens. He is suddenly gripped by an unearthly composure. On that night, he made Wembley seem like a training ground on a Tuesday morning.

Ziegler's penalty was like an improved version of Reuter's. Four-all. If Teddy Sheringham could score then Germany were facing sudden death. All in all, the first four English penalties had been faultless. The same players had done the job against Spain, and so well that the fifth, Sheringham, was not then called upon. Now it was his turn. Kopke came off his line so early, so blatantly, that it looked as if he wanted to beat Sheringham to the tackle. Throughout his career, the England striker has made use of a feint – falsely throwing up one or even both of his arms – that is so regular that it has become part of his personality, like Gascoigne's neck jerks. He can barely receive a pass without an arm semaphoring a fake movement. When I played football as a kid, and I mean when I was ten or eleven, everyone – professionals, Sunday players, schoolkids – performed this trick. Like everyone else in my school, I would do it whenever I got the chance, which was whenever I got the ball. I probably also did it when I didn't have the ball, just to keep my hand in, so to speak. It was a seventies move, a seventies conceit. I don't know who started it – perhaps George Best – but the dummy arm was as much part of the time as round collars and industrial action. Now Sheringham is the only player in the world, as far as I know, who does it. A quaint anachronism, it can make him look primly dated. But the extraordinary thing is, it works. Defenders buy Sheringham's feint as if it were going out of stock, which, in a way, it is. And Kopke bought it, too.

Kuntz. He had equalised for Germany during their fifteen minutes of dominance after Shearer had scored. Now he had the opportunity to end England's 'thirty years of pain' and put them – us – into the final. The chance was ruthlessly spurned. He drove the ball high to Seaman's left as the keeper went right.

In his confessional autobiography, *Addicted*, Tony Adams opens at this suffocating moment. 'We had not actually planned for this,' he recalls. 'For penalties, yes, but not going beyond the first five . . .' The thinking, presumably, in not planning beyond the five penalty specialists was so as not to put unnecessary pressure on those players who were to follow. The other point is that the coach might have wanted to wait to see who was 'up for it' come the time. If that was the case, I detect a flaw. I think it's better not to look for volunteers but to have a set running-list that only changes if a player is substituted or says that he is not confident. That way, you avoid the heroic but futile gesture.

In a diary he wrote for the *Guardian* at the time, Gareth Southgate said that he was notionally placed at number nine for penalty-taking against Spain. 'If it had gone as far as me it wouldn't have been a problem. I hope. I've taken one before, for Crystal Palace at Ipswich. It was 2-2 in the eighty-ninth minute,

I hit the post and we went down that year. But I think I'd be far more comfortable now than I was then.'

In the space of four days, he jumped three positions in the pecking order. Adams went on to write: 'I have never been a great penalty-taker myself, and although I would have taken one if others had declined, as had happened with Arsenal in a European Cup Winners' Cup semi-final against Sampdoria the previous year, I was in no rush to volunteer. Gareth, bravely, fatefully, was.'

Sometimes that wise cautionary advice 'Don't just do something – stand there' has its place in life. Whether this was right occasion to make use of it is debatable. Someone had to take the penalty. In fact, Adams was the only player in the team – apart from the nominated first five – who had scored a penalty as a professional footballer. Paul Ince, Steve McManaman and Darren Anderton, the other three outfield players, were penalty virgins. And Seaman had taken one against Manchester United in the 1993 FA Charity Shield, which Peter Schmeichel saved. I've heard it said that Venables was not aware of Southgate's zero per cent record from the spot, and that had he been he would have reconsidered the centre-back's position in the order. Idle, pointless conjecture, of course, but taking into account the all-or-nothing nature of penalties, one might think a player's penalty history should be part of the decision process.

Southgate was in no danger of hitting the post this time. He shaped as if to put the ball to the keeper's left but he stroked it marginally to his right. Kopke moved later than he had done on any of the previous shots, which was still early, but not very far off his line. He didn't need to. The ball was hit so tamely that it would have been difficult for Kopke not to save it. So he did the easy thing instead.

'Why didn't you just belt it?' Southgate's mother would ask. I think it was enough that he didn't belt her.

Throughout the tournament, Southgate seemed to place himself effortlessly in the right position. Now, for the first time, he was lost. He looked as if he could no longer breathe in air, as if an atomic change had taken place around him, depriving him of oxygen. Pearce was the first to him. 'When I went up to him,' Pearce said afterwards, 'I told him, "We are all in in it together: that's how we play the game."'

Byatt wrote that she hated penalty shoot-outs because they 'turn the beauty of the group into confrontation between individuals'. Pearce let Southgate know that he was still part of the group. And his, I feel, was a statement that conveyed its own moral beauty.

'We came in with collective responsibility,' said Venables, 'and went out the same way. He's a man. He wanted to take the penalty. He did what Stuart Pearce did. That which doesn't kill you makes you stronger. He will be better for it. You saw what a thrill it gave Stuart Pearce after missing all those years ago. I'm sure Gareth will do the same.'

Not yet. Venables was more accurate in his Nietzschean prediction. Southgate would later say that he 'felt a much stronger person' because of the experience. Indeed, I'm sure that the personal growth was so rewarding that Southgate would not have wanted Andreas Moller to miss out on the experience as well. Rather than develop as a man, Moller simply scored a goal. He achieved it by doing something that no German had done for a long while. He hit the ball at the dead centre of the target. Seaman, perhaps swayed by

Moller's left arm, dived right. If he had stayed where he was, he would have saved the ball at face height. If. If. Nearly. Nearly . . .

That night there were skirmishes and attacks across the country and a small riot erupted in Trafalgar Square. 'I actually received a letter from someone', Southgate told *On the Spot*, 'that said I'm appearing at Kensington nick on the fifteenth of July and it's your fault.'

A good friend of mine was stabbed in the face with a screwdriver. A teenager was knifed in Brighton because he was suspected – wrongly – of being German. And Tony Adams embarked on his lowest and last drinking session that was to lead to his successful attempt to confront and overcome his addiction. None of those events had anything to do with Southgate. Only the most enfeebled minds could possibly think otherwise. He was responsible simply for missing a penalty. But in an effort to protect Southgate from enfeebled minds, a sentimental consensus was formed within football which refused to accept that he was responsible for missing the penalty. Instead the penalty was made responsible for its random torture. Anyone could have missed, became the approved line, and it just so happened to be him. The questions of how or why he missed were deemed too obvious or too insensitive to ask. If it had nothing to do with technique, what was it about? How bizarre that something as straightforward as a penalty could be seen as so mysterious, and that something so precise could be treated with such vagueness. The result was that, if Euro '96 offered any lessons about the psychology of the shoot-out, they were allowed to go largely unlearned.

CHAPTER FOUR

Negativity

In his classic work of magical realism, *My World Cup Story*, Glenn Hoddle wrote: 'England's players had never been as well prepared for any game as they were for the match against Argentina.' The England coach was right in many respects. In terms of vitamin and mineral intake, for example, the team that walked on to the pitch in St Etienne on that soft June evening in 1998 was methodically and comprehensively supplemented. In matters of what Hoddle called 'spiritual cleansing', Eileen Drewery's hands had worked hard to ensure that the players' spirits were sparklingly clean. And months of protracted negotiations with Paul Smith, the fashion designer, had already delivered a sartorial coup for Hoddle. Rather than arriving in a dark-coloured suit, the team had stepped off the plane in France wearing a far more summery beige number. In all the key areas, it seemed, England were a lesson in readiness. The only detail that escaped Hoddle's meticulous preparations was the minor issue of penalties.

True, the three previous knock-out games in which England competed had all ended in shoot-outs. And the two games prior to that had also come within minutes of being resolved by penalties (in a sense, of course, one of those games, against Cameroon, was decided on Lineker's two penalties). Pedants might also add that in the two World Cups before France, seven out of the thirty knock-out games finished with penalty shoot-outs: almost one in four. At Euro '96, four out of the seven knock-out games were still not settled at the end of extra time. Add those three competitions together and that's thirty per cent of international knock-out games going to penalties. But was all that enough reason to institute a few minutes of penalty practice for the whole squad? The Argentinians thought so. They had arranged penalty competitions in their own training sessions. England, however, who had lost two semi-finals in recent years on penalties, did not include penalty-taking in theirs. There was, for the record, some penalty-*saving* involved. The three England goalkeepers were shown videos of Argentinian penalties. Hoddle noticed that Batistuta had put his recent penalties to the keeper's right and warned his men accordingly. Seaman, famously, does not decide which way to go until he sees the player run up. Against Argentina, he had to make that decision only six minutes into the game, when England conceded a penalty. In the event Seaman went right, as did Batistuta, and got a hand to the ball, although he could not prevent it from going in. Hoddle claimed that the homework had proved vital in the nearly save. 'That's where your preparation comes in,' wrote the England coach.

Actually, there was one other area of penalties that Hoddle deemed worthy of attention: how to be awarded them. Before Batistuta converted, Diego Simeone, the Argentine captain, demonstrated the art of conning the referee inside the penalty box. Racing on to a diagonal ball that was too far in front of him to control or even strike, Simeone was going nowhere fast. Seaman nevertheless rushed out and slid towards the ball to collect it in his arms. Just before the keeper made contact, Simeone nicked the ball away with his toe. Realising he wasn't going to get the ball, Seaman immediately pulled his arms away, but his body's momentum meant that he gained the faintest touch on the Argentinian, who made no attempt to avoid him. Down went Simeone, as if caught by a sniper. When the penalty kick was first introduced, the rule was seen by many as an insult to sportsmanship, as it assumed that players intended to foul their opponents. Yet there was no suggestion in the no-holds-barred days of the nineteenth century that a player would ever wilfully attempt to influence the referee. Simeone got up and mimed taking a card out of his pocket, in a successful effort to have Seaman cautioned. This was the act, as was another Simeone later performed, of a cad of the most unscrupulous kidney.

Hoddle had given his players strict instructions on what to do in the penalty area: 'I have told players,' he told one reporter, 'if they get knocked or get fouled then they go down.' A few minutes after Simeone went over, Michael Owen ran at speed towards Roberto Ayala, the Argentinian sweeper who was standing on the edge of the penalty area. Owen pushed the ball past Ayala and headed directly for him. The defender had no option but to stand aside, which he did, his hands raised in defeat. Owen, who would not have got to the ball, went crashing to the ground. If there was contact it was between the hairs of the players' legs. The referee again awarded a penalty. He didn't book Ayala, though, which moved Hoddle to instruct Ince to protest. 'One of the biggest negatives to come out of the tournament,' Hoddle later wrote in his book, 'was that too many players seemed to be encouraged by the new directives to get their opponents booked by diving. It's a habit that is creeping into the game and one that should be stamped out fast.' Through some kind of moral time warp, which even Hoddle would struggle to comprehend, the referee must have anticipated these words. He booked Ince for trying to get Ayala booked.

'What was important to me,' said Hoddle after the match, 'was that [Owen] did what he should have done in trying to get the penalty. That is how we play.' Later, cushioned by time and presumably his ghost-writer, David Davies, then the Football Association's PR man, Hoddle amended his view slightly. 'There's no way I would ever tell a player to go down in the box, to dive in order to earn a penalty. What I would tell him is that if an opponent physically catches you then stay on your feet if you can; if not, if you've been fouled, go down. That's professionalism.'

The inherent contradictions and fudging of that statement are too typical and dreary to analyse. What captures the eye is the comic use of 'professionalism'. The abuse of that word is not new, although the punishment has taken on a different form of late. So-called professional fouls used to be popular when I was a kid. Basically, this meant fouls that were blatant, that looked, in a word, amateurish. Most often professional fouls were committed when a striker was through on goal, at which point a defender would bring him down in the most flagrant and ruthless manner he could think of. There was no subtlety to the offence, no mark of professional skill or seasoned practice. Belatedly, the rule-makers took steps to outlaw such tackles and those who committed them earned a mandatory sending-off. That's when the professionals moved into the diving business. Nowadays, with the conspicuous exception of Robbie Fowler, attackers seem to spend half the game looking for penalties. And understandably, because nobody knows when they might be given. As TV analysis becomes more intrusive and the game more competitive, the penalty award has become a game in itself. As many as half the penalties that are awarded should not be, and for every penalty that is awarded two more should be and are not. So much is heard about the randomness of the shoot-out but it is the winning of the penalty, not scoring of it, that is the true lottery. There is, as so few in football are willing to accept, nothing arbitrary about scoring a penalty kick. It is a skill. Get it right and you always score. Get it wrong, and you might not.

Alan Shearer had not taken a competitive penalty for almost eighteen months when he found himself in the position to put England level against Argentina. Not that you would have noticed. Hard and high to the keeper's right, his shot made Roa, the Argentine keeper, look like an irrelevant prop. *That*, as if we needed reminding, is where your preparation comes in.

In one way or another, the match was plotted by penalties. But it would be miserably wrong to say that they were its only story. Just as Diego Maradona's slalom run leading to his second goal against England in

1986 helped clear the 'Hand of God' stink of his first, so did Owen's strike overshadow his contribution to England's first. An irresistible goal of deathless beauty, it very nearly rivalled Maradona's – and that is the highest praise. The game swung to and fro, and Argentina equalised with a brilliantly cheeky free kick on the stroke of half-time. Shortly after the break, an incident took place which transformed the nature of the game but not, as has often been implied, the result. Simeone clattered into the back of David Beckham and then kneeled on him as he got up. Beckham responded by blindly flicking out a boot that caught Simeone. Again Simeone found the vertical position an excruciating impossibility and duly hit the deck screaming.

Beckham was sent off and Simeone was booked. I still feel, as I did at the time, that the Danish referee was indulging in the most arrant and misguided of liberal impulses: punish the victim. It was as if a mugger had been fined for assault and his victim imprisoned for slapping him. While the issue has no direct bearing on penalties, I'm going into detail here because of how this event was later identified as the cause of England's demise, not least by Hoddle himself. And

NEGATIVITY

Beckham, atrociously, was made the scapegoat. Here is Ian Wright, a fellow squad member: 'Without being too harsh on David, it cost us the game.' (One wonders what Wright would say if he were to be harsh.) David Lacey, writing in the *Guardian*, suggested that anyone who cared would be 'cursing the day Beckham was born'. The tabloids really went to town: 'Moment of Lunacy that Cost Cup Hopes' ran the front page of the *Daily Mail*, and '10 Heroic Lions One Stupid Boy' was the *Daily Mirror*'s offering. By the way, it's worth mentioning the change in press coverage that was triggered eight years before by Gazza's tears. Back in 1990, England's progress in the tournament earned them no more than a back page in the broadsheets, and sometimes less, and not a great deal more in the tabloids. In 1998 the *Daily Telegraph*, a newspaper that had long viewed football as suspiciously plebeian, devoted practically its whole front page to England's game with Argentina. Every paper had two match reporters and the tabloids were filled with football from front to back. All that coverage needed a story and the story was that Beckham was to blame. 'David Beckham's sending off cost us dearly,'

Hoddle claimed that night. 'I am not denying it cost us the game.'

In the wake of the tabloid-led vilification of Beckham, Hoddle sweetened his comments by saying that nobody should be blamed. Yet he returned once more to the theme in his book: 'I couldn't get away from my belief that we'd have won the World Cup if we'd have beaten Argentina, and no one on this earth will ever change my opinion that if we'd had eleven men on the pitch we'd have won that game.' If that appears diplomatically impersonal, Hoddle makes his point even clearer: 'If he [Beckham] hadn't got sent off we'd have had eleven men on the pitch and would have won the game – I was convinced of that.' In other words, if it was not for Beckham's indiscretion England would have won the World Cup.

The amazing thing about this thinking is that it was shared by so many people. To recap: the score was level at 2-2 when Beckham was sent off. Argentina had just scored a morale-sapping equaliser. *No one on this earth* can say what would have happened had Beckham not kicked Simeone. But we do know that the score was also 2-2 when open play came to a finish. The fact that it remained

unchanged had much to do with an inde-
fatigable defensive performance by England
and a concomitant loss of attacking ideas by
Argentina. Both sides seemed affected by the
sending-off, but England's response was, in a
defensive sense, the more positive.

The whole two hours, not to mention the
shoot-out, were, if anything, even more
enthralling than the two epic encounters with
Germany. And it did not go unnoticed
elsewhere in the world. In Italy, *La Repubblica*
offered its appreciation: '. . . a magnificent
thing, a living picture of men and feelings . . .
this is what football should be: cinema without a script, a melodrama where the libretto
and the finale are written by the singers
directly on stage, with their voices and their
imaginations.'

Le Monde in France compared Owen to
Leonardo DiCaprio: 'He's all that's needed to
restore the image of England, which we are
too inclined to see as a production line of
tattooed, alcoholic and dangerous hooligans.'

The English press, in contrast, focused on
Beckham. They would have done so anyway,
but I think that Hoddle, consciously or not,
was culpable here. He had to find a reason for
England's defeat because, as we know, he

believed fervently in predestination. So convinced was he that England's fate was to win the World Cup, there had to be an explanation for the unforeseen outcome that resonated with transcendental meaning. The mundane fact that England scored fewer penalties than Argentina would not do. Hoddle's account of an unrelated story throws light on his superstitious thinking, an irrationality that football by its very nature seems to encourage. Early in England's preparations Gareth Southgate was involved in a 'freak accident' which left him with a jarred ankle. Hoddle was furious until he realised that it would enable him to try out Gary Neville in Southgate's place. 'The idea that there might have been a reason for the injury', recalled Hoddle, 'improved my mood slightly.' Of course, there was a reason for Southgate's injury: he slipped over when trying to get to a pass from David Batty. But that wasn't *the* reason, the karmic reason on whose principles the universe is organised.

Throughout *My World Cup Story*, Hoddle litters the narrative with signs that seem to confirm England's victorious destiny. There are almost as many references to omens and gut feelings as there are exclamations marks – and Hoddle and Davies are men who are resolutely unafraid of exclamatory punctuation. In *Addicted*, Tony Adams remembers the build-up to the crucial pre-tournament qualifying game against Italy. 'Each morning I sat under a tree reading *The Celestine Prophecy* by James Redfield, a book about meditation, human insight and spirituality. It was eerie, because I noticed Glenn Hoddle was reading it too.'

Who could have prophesied Beckham's sending-off? Eileen Drewery was not in France at that time, as Hoddle later bitterly regretted. Drewery, he felt, could have administered physical and mental healing and, one supposes, prevented the psychic scarring that made Beckham vulnerable to provocation. In Hoddle's conception of the world only such a haphazard disaster could have disrupted the natural flow of fate. 'I don't know if it was destiny,' said Hoddle after the game, 'everything just went against us.' Yet, following Beckham's sending off, England could be said to be unlucky in only one respect. In extra time Jose Chamot, the Argentine defender, punched the ball in his own penalty area. England should have been awarded a penalty. They weren't and so the referee allowed another meaninglessly common injustice, the kind which most teams feel they suffer at some point in a game. The 'goal' that Sol Campbell scored a few minutes from full time was correctly ruled-out for the simple reason that Shearer elbowed the keeper. Whether Campbell would have scored without the intervention of the England captain's unfunny humerus is a moot question. I happen to think he would have done. But none of that mattered when England lined up to take penalties in the shoot-out.

Hoddle maintains that his team of '98 was better than Venables's team of '96. Michael Owen and David Beckham would be welcome additions, I would say, to any team in world football, so therefore Hoddle, in an abstract sense, has a point. By what criteria do you judge a team, though, other than success? Venables came closer to success than Hoddle and part of the reason he did so is because his team practised penalties. None of his nominated penalty-takers missed a penalty in the two shoot-outs of Euro '96. Where Venables erred was in not preparing for a shoot-out that went beyond the first five. With Germany, you have to go all the way. Hoddle did not have to worry about that with Argentina. Nevertheless he was somewhat hampered in the penalty department by the absence of Beckham, who, Hoddle has said, would have been selected in the first five, and the tactical substitutions resulting from playing with ten men – in particular the replacement of Darren Anderton by David Batty. Adams, for one, could not see the value in that decision. 'I know Glenn had a balancing act between wanting to win it in open play and maybe playing for penalties, but I think we would have been better off putting on another attacking player, as the back four was looking nice and solid anyway.'

Hoddle has since acknowledged that he was playing for penalties in extra time, although he has also said that he was going for the win. In any case, I think Robert Lee, who possessed a fine shot and had scored a penalty while playing for Newcastle, would have made more sense as Anderton's replacement than Batty. When the whistle blew at the end of extra time, there were only three players available for England that Hoddle felt confident would score penalties: Alan Shearer, Paul Merson and Michael Owen. 'We had not practised penalties in training,' wrote Adams, 'except for Alan Shearer, who always likes to. I wonder if there is anything that prepares you for the ordeal.

However, I believe that they should have been rehearsed, especially after our Euro '96 experience, but nobody had suggested it at the end of training the previous day.'

The irony is that most of the players spent their spare time, of which there was no shortage, practising on the golf course. There was nothing remiss about that. Relaxation is a fundamental aspect of preparation. The thought persists, however, that if the Argentinian game had been decided on putting a golfball rather than kicking a football, then England would have coasted into the next round.

Hoddle would put England's failure at penalties down to a historical lack of success. 'Too many things go through your mind if you keep losing at penalties,' he said afterwards. 'If you keep winning them, like the Germans, psychologically they feel that it is going to go their way. The confidence is there . . . It's just a mental thing.'

Once again, Hoddle had a valid premise and an invalid conclusion, which was essentially to ignore penalties. England are not the only team to have a poor record in shoot-outs. Italy's statistics are even less enviable. During the nineties, they lost the quarter-final,

NEGATIVITY

semi-final and final of three World Cups on penalties. And, in the same period, Holland lost the quarter-final and semi-final of the European Championships and a semi-final of the World Cup on penalties. If you were looking for national clichés to explain the problem, then the Italians' supposedly hot-blooded passion is perhaps not the ideal temperament for a shoot-out. And the Dutch tendency to divide into squabbling cliques is equally ill-suited to the in-it-together mentality that, paradoxically, makes the individuality of penalties a collective concern. A more acceptable assessment of the plight of the English, Dutch and Italian national squads is that failure does, in some way, become inscribed on the DNA of a football team, even though the actual players change. Dr Sik says it's not unlike hearing that a friend has been stuck in a lift. Suddenly, you become slightly phobic yourself about the idea of stepping in one. The way to overcome phobias, as any psychologist will tell you, is to confront them, demystify them, take the terror away. England did confront their fear of the penalty at Euro '96, but unfortunately, to mix metaphobes, their lift came to halt between the fifth and sixth floor.

ON PENALTIES

One player who had no intention of confronting his teammates' fear, let alone his own, in '96 was, of course, Paul Ince. He had given another magnificent performance for England in St Etienne, destroying Argentina's midfield manoeuvres and then powering his team forwards on the break. At the beginning of that spookily timeless period between the end of extra time and the start of the shoot-out, Ince slumped to the ground.

Hoddle said after the match: 'David Batty and Paul Ince said they wanted to take a penalty. When you get a positive vibe from a player, you've got to go with it. The five who wanted to take them were up for it.'

The implication is that Batty and Ince volunteered. That is not strictly accurate. As Batty later explained: 'When it came to picking five penalty-takers we were a bit short of attacking players, so I think he [Hoddle] went for the experienced lads. I was quite happy to take one.'

With Batty on board, Hoddle walked over to Ince, whose body language, lying slurred on the ground, did not say 'up for it'.

'We need one,' implored Hoddle. 'We need one. Go on, Paul.'

Ince stood up and Hoddle, relieved, gave

him a comradely pat on the back. How could Ince, 'the Guv'nor', say no? He had not been allowed to forget his stance at Euro '96. His critics had labelled him a coward, although none, as far as I am aware, to his face. 'Some players feel they have to do it,' says Dr Sik. 'Ince is a classic example. He felt like he had to do it, but you can tell that he didn't want to.'

Once on his feet, Ince set about getting into his role, like a method actor inhabiting his character. He walked around geeing up other players, slapping backs, bearing his teeth in an expression of toughed-up conviction. But the effect was a long way from convincing. To be brave is to act brave because the very notion of bravery presupposes the existence of fear; fear that must be quelled or hidden. Ince's staunch exterior could not conceal the vulnerability he was feeling and that made his performance almost as touching as it was worrying.

Hoddle has said that Ince wanted to go second. We must assume this is because he had an impatient desire to bring his part in the ordeal to an end. Shearer, naturally, was always going to go first. Hoddle decided the running order would be Shearer, Ince, Merson, Owen, Batty. After that came Gary

Neville, Gareth Southgate and, then, Tony Adams, Sol Campbell and, finally, if it came to it, David Seaman. Adams, again the only successful penalty-taker in the lower half, acknowledged that he was 'ever the reluctant penalty-taker through ability rather than attitude, though afterwards I did moment-arily feel a bit guilty that I hadn't stepped forward'.

At the end of extra time, Southgate was asked by one of Hoddle's assistants, Ray Clemence, how he would feel if penalties went to sudden death. 'I was fine with it,' Southgate later said. 'I felt more confident than the first time round. I realised that it was genuinely a lottery.'

The denial that the England team was in appeared endemic. 'I never thought I'd have to take one [a penalty] in a penalty shoot-out,' Batty admitted afterwards. Had these players not been taking any notice of the past decade? Did they think that Shearer was just ex-tremely lucky in the international lottery of penalty-taking?

Shearer, needless to say, was lucky once again. He levelled the score with another unanswerable strike, after Sergio Berti, a penalty-specialist who had been brought on for Simeone, had opened the Argentine account with a fine shot low into Seaman's left-hand corner. If ever there was a case-book example of a man showing his nerves it was Hernan Crespo, another substitute, and the second Argentinian penalty-taker. That he had lost the mental battle with Seaman was evident long before he kicked the ball. He looked like an uncertain fifteen-year-old preparing to ask the class babe for a date. Breathing appeared difficult, his mouth was taut with stress and you could almost see his heart beating beneath his shirt. Seaman went early to his left and met Crespo's shot at a comfortable height about five feet in from the post. The Argentinian, later to become briefly the world's most expensive player, looked strangely relieved; depressed as well, but no longer unmanned by anxiety. The worst was over. His urge to get it done had over-whelmed his need to score.

Now Hoddle regretted his running order. 'If I'd known that David Seaman was going to make an early save in the penalty shoot-out, giving us the chance to take the lead, I'd have had one of our experienced takers at number two in the order.' Presumably he meant Merson. At seventeen, Owen could not be described as experienced.

'It is on that walk from the halfway line,' Hoddle said, 'where a player knows whether he is going to miss it.' Did Ince know? You felt as if he at least suspected his fate. The positive vibe of which Hoddle spoke was not registering on my television set. I could see the John Wayne stride, the determined bounce that Ince gave the ball, I saw the attempt at a smile that Ince tried before his upper lip gave way. But the ions around the Guv'nor were the wrong charge. He was giving out what Hoddle would call 'negativity'. A man who routinely walked down the tunnel before each game of football without his shirt on, as Ince did, would have dangerously little immunity to the superstition surrounding shoot-outs. I had not a scintilla of doubt that Ince would find the goalkeeper. His shot was uncannily similar to Crespo's, as if he'd studied it and said: 'I can do that.' The only difference was that Ince signalled his side-foot even more plainly. He shuffled slightly in his run-up, but it did not throw Roa. The goalkeeper was over a yard off his line when Ince's foot made impact. The linesman, or assistant referee, might just as well have been inspecting the dirt under his fingernails for all the use he made of his – seemingly decorative – position adjacent to the goal-line.

Veron's shot was a replica of Shearer's: hard in the roof of the net and to the keeper's right. Two-one. Merson had to suffer the distraction of Roa rightly protesting that the ball was not on the spot. The referee, who had a poor game, seemed to have a *laissez-faire* approach to the geometry of the penalty: the keeper was allowed off his line and the ball off its spot. He booked Roa. Merson composed himself and fired the ball to the right of the Argentinian, who managed to get his left hand to it but could not prevent a goal. Seaman could not have stopped Galliano's kick – although he was inches from it – by diving along the goal-line. However, had he come out in the manner of Roa, I think he may just have done.

Owen, the impishly confident marksman, looked as if he was walking up to win a coconut at a school fate. Hoddle had said that the teenager was not a natural goalscorer, a statement which was greeted with derision in many quarters of the press. One of the qualities I admired in Hoddle was his determination to show the press that they were a secondary or even tertiary concern. The job of England manager has become so caught up in the machinations of public relations that many journalists have grown quite unabashed in declaring that the first priority of the coach is to give them copy. In reality, as Sir Alf Ramsey proved, you can maintain an obvious contempt for the press just so long as you win, in which case it becomes impolite to remember your more questionable pronouncements. Hoddle, who had said many silly things, was always going to come unstuck with the media, but he was not wrong about Owen. There was nothing natural about his goalscoring talent or his nerveless guile. They were unnatural, supernatural.

The line between triumph and disaster in sport is exquisitely thin and unforgivingly rigid. Owen's shot hit the inside of Roa's right-hand post and went in. A few inches the other side and it would have rebounded out. Then the story would have been about a young kid cracking under pressure. As it was, most commentators concluded that Owen was aiming for the inside of the post. This begs the question: if it's possible to be accurate to a matter of inches, how can another player be inaccurate to a matter of yards?

Ayala's penalty proved that you don't have to hit a ball hard to score, you just need to place it in the right spot. He practically made a pass into the unreachable space between the end of Seaman's dive and his left-hand post. Four-three. Now it was sudden death.

'David Batty juggled the ball as he approached the penalty spot,' wrote Richard Williams in the *Guardian*, 'like a man wanting to show an insouciance he didn't feel.'

Oh the weird workings of the mind. Batty *did* feel a kind of insouciance, or a kind of out-of-body confidence. Why else would he have changed his mind and decided to place rather than blast the ball? He has stated that he was confident. Except he also said this about penalty-taking: 'I'd taken one in a junior game and I missed that, so I wasn't full of confidence.' Who knows? Probably not even Batty himself. Is it even possible to recall thoughts that are the product of such mental intensity? Can you separate what you think from what you think you think or what you think you should think? Batty's shot was like a mirror reverse of Ince's. Roa was off so early he almost had to turn back, as Batty had misplaced the ball too near the centre of goal. But he found the ball as surely as he later found God (and retired from the game). The Yorkshireman gave a little skip as he completed his shot, a heart-breaking jump of shock and dire recognition, a brief dance of death.

'That's the first penalty I've ever been asked to take,' said Batty as the post-mortem got underway. 'I've never even taken one in training.'

When I heard those words a memory came back to me. At first, I wasn't sure if I had imagined it or willed it into being out of sheer frustration and unwillingness to accept the truth. But I tentatively asked others and they confirmed that they, too, had the same recovered memory. Was it some kind of folk memory or mass hysteria? I couldn't find any record of what I thought I remembered in the newspapers but it still persisted, stronger now even than it was then. I vividly recall Hoddle talking about how his squad would practise penalties. Goalkeepers would be tested from ten yards, while penalty-takers would deliver their shots from fourteen yards. I also recall thinking what a good idea that was. (David O'Leary, the Leeds manager, and himself a successful penalty-taker for Ireland at Italia '90, said that his players practise penalties and that the taker has to inform the keeper which way he is going to put the ball before shooting. I think that's an even better idea, because the secret of penalties is to evade the keeper's maximum dive, not to guess which way he is not going to go. That said, Leeds still lost to Leicester in that monster effort.)

'Of course we put in a certain amount of practice,' Hoddle stated in his World Cup memoir:

> But you can never recreate on the training ground the circumstances of a real shoot-out. I know – I've taken penalties in Cup finals . . . When you run up, and that goal starts shrinking, then you know you're in trouble. Unfortunately you don't know how you are going to feel until that moment of truth. Frankly, you've either got it, or you haven't . . .

> Practising until kingdom come isn't necessarily the answer. In fact, it might just make things worse; we don't want to build an even higher mental wall. Of course, it's my job to come up with the answer, and it

needs a lot of thought.

The fourteen-yard sessions never material-ised. According to a number of players, not least Batty and Adams, Shearer was the only player to practise penalties. In the immediate aftermath of England's exit, Hoddle was very defensive about his lack of preparation. 'I'm not denying practice does help,' he said. 'A golfer can practise a thousand putts on the putting green. But he can then go out on the last day of a tournament when there's thirty thousand there and miss. If it was all down to practice and it always went in for you, then it would be a simple scenario. It isn't like that.'

Who ever suggested that it was? The alter-native is to do nothing, accept that penalties are a lottery and see what happens. So far, that policy has not worked.

CHAPTER FIVE

I Could Do That

As I turned to face perhaps the finest penalty-saving goalkeeper in the business, my thoughts were not entirely untroubled by doubt or regret. Absurdly, this was going to be only the second spot kick I had ever taken – the first being some twenty-seven years ago. Despite all my theories about practice, and my reservations about the England team's lax attitude towards penalties, I found myself having opted for the David Batty method of preparation: no preparation. In fact, I had taken the laid-back approach to training to new extremes of indolence. After a two-year lay-off from the game, I had still not managed to get around to kicking a ball. This was to be by my first touch. There were reasons for the neglect, some of which I shall try to explain, but just then I could not afford to dwell on setbacks. I needed to be positive. And, without wishing to boast, there was good cause to be positive. I had scored from that penalty three decades before.

It wasn't just any penalty, either. Television cameras were there to record the event. In the 1972–73 season I was playing for my class team in what was then known as the fourth year at Rhyl Street primary school in Kentish Town, north London. Actually, every boy in my class played for the team. Selection was based solely on being in my class and not a girl. Thinking about it, some notion of choice is implicit in the word 'selection', whereas it was really no less than a draft. Not that I needed to be coerced. Had it been up to me, I would have played football right through the day from getting up to going to bed. The rest of my life and school were, as far as I could see, just the unavoidable bits in between. Our greatest rivals – strictly speaking, our only rivals – were the team from the other class in the fourth year. We played them each morning before school and every lunchtime – or 'dinnertime' as we called it then.

The games took place on what was known as a 'bomb debris site' about a hundred yards from the school. My ten-year-old self, I now realise, was located exactly halfway between

the present day and the end of the Second
World War. And, as incredible as it now
seems, there were still areas of London in the
early seventies that were scarred by bomb
damage. Unbeknown to us, the wasteland on
which we played had become the focus of a
struggle between an idealistic hippie organisation that wanted to develop a community
centre there and, I think, the local council,
which owned the site. Anyway, Thames
Television became interested and sent along a
reporter and cameraman to do a story.

When we arrived at the clearing to resume
the daily contest with our implacable opponents, the media were waiting. 'Listen,' said
the bloke with camera, 'don't take any notice
of us. Just play your normal game.' As a child,
you get used to adults making hopeful
statements – 'The weather's bound to clear up
later' or 'I'm going to leave the room and
when I return I expect to see the stolen pencil
case on my desk' – but this was another order
of optimism. Some of my classmates didn't
even have televisions, so the idea of them
affecting to treat a television camera with
nonchalant indifference was a study in
bespoke futility.

Our 'normal game' usually resulted in a

score of, say, 13-11 or 18-14. Goals were not a problem. There was no precedent for a nil-nil draw. But due to the manic need to shine in front of the camera, the match was goalless with a couple of minutes to go. No one passed the ball. In itself, this was not out of the ordinary. Passing had always been an extreme option, resorted to only when you had run out of pitch or puff. The difference now was that whenever anyone had the ball everyone tried to tackle him, the opposition *and* his own teammates. Scoring a goal was not the point. Getting into frame was the only concern.

And then somebody – perhaps fooled by my pre-Sheringham feint – clattered into me in the penalty box. I can't remember through what powers of arbitration a penalty was awarded, only that it was. I was recently reminded of the ensuing scene by the altercations that took place between the West Ham players Paulo di Canio and Frank Lampard, when their team was awarded a penalty against Bradford City. Both men wanted to take the kick and both put their hands on the ball. They stood face-to-face and argued it out, neither prepared to back down, until finally their manager Harry Redknapp, doubtless aware that such delaying tactics are less effective when you're behind in a game, signalled that di Canio should take the kick alone.

Imagine that situation multiplied by ten or more, and without the intervention of a Redknapp, and you'll begin to realise what I had to go through to gain what was rightfully mine – I was, after all, the one who had been fouled. My unswerving determination was borne of the certain knowledge that if I scored, the penalty – the game's only goal – would be shown later that evening on television. On television, where Tottenham Hotspur and Manchester United appeared. On television. In colour.

Having eventually wrestled the ball away from the mêlée and placed it on the spot, I then experienced a moment of dizzying self-consciousness. I could feel the camera focusing on my sweating brow, boring into my private insecurities, reading my every intention. Although ignorant of the concept of cognitive behaviourism, I knew I had to collect myself, banish these thoughts from my mind and concentrate on the job in hand. What we liked most about the strip of tarmac on the bomb debris site were its goalposts.

They made a game seem real, grown-up, almost professional. Now as I looked up from the ball, the idea of seeing it fly between those posts grabbed hold of me like some sacred vision. 'Keep your head down,' said a voice inside me. I ran up and cracked the thing as hard as I could. Such was my resolve to obey the injunction that I did not look up in time to be sure whether the ball had gone in or not. But my success was confirmed by my class-mates shouting and racing after me. I had, of course, already taken off, consumed by the glory of the moment and the adulation of the camera and the instinct to run. They say, the pros, that they don't know what happens to them in the seconds after scoring a goal. They don't know what they're doing. Don't believe it. Even in a state of advanced ecstasy I was keen to make my celebration correspond to those I had watched live and on television: a gripped fist held aloft, as I sped round in a smiling semi-circle of joy.

When I got home, I told everyone and we gathered round to watch the report after the six o'clock news. There was an interminable interview with some or other faceless bureau-crat, followed by an even longer one with a well-meaning long-hair. Cut to a three-second shot of a few indistinguishable kids – but definitely not including me – walking across the tarmac, and then back to the stiff and the freak moaning on. And that was it. No penalty. No goal. No television fame. At such a tender age, I had experienced the special pressures of the penalty kick and the ruthless demands of television. Who, then, could have guessed that they were made for each other?

Bob Wilson was, if anything, even more enthusiastic about my taking penalties against David Seaman than I was. He spoke in excited awe of the Arsenal and England number one's commanding presence. 'He's a huge guy,' said Bob. 'It always surprises people when they meet him.' He warned of Seaman's secret means of reading the penalty-taker's run-up. 'You have to be careful. David will never reveal his system.' I listened to it all with the nerveless assurance of a man who could not conceive of shrinking from the challenge. I know it sounds churlish, but as a Spurs fan, I relished the prospect – no, the inevitability – of sending Seaman the wrong way. So what if he was huge? That just meant there was more of him that he had to get down. Would that ever-present walrus grin still be intact after I had rocketed ten penalties past him? I doubted it.

As agreed, I called Bob a week after my visit. Once past the usual preliminaries – I had to remind him who I was and then delicately discourage him from reversing my name so that it resembled that of an actor who once played a mincing fop in *Brideshead Revisited* – I mentioned the Seaman encounter.

'What?' said Bob, blankly.

'What did, er, David think?' I ventured.

'About what?'

'You know, about the, er, penalties.'

'What penalties?' asked Bob, still some way from comprehension.

'Well, erm, the penalties we discussed last week. You remember, I was going to take a few against him.'

'Oh, *that*,' said Bob, briskly up to pace. 'No, he can't do it. Insurance.'

'Sorry?'

'What if you were to break his finger?'

Of course.

'Bob,' I nearly said, 'there's no need to explain. Who can blame Dave for bottling it.'

Sure, he may, for all I know, have faced Matthew Elliot and Roberto Carlos, guys who, granted, can stick a little pace on a ball.

But his anxiety about standing twelve yards from a man who really knew how to put boot to leather was not in the least bit surprising. He was, I assumed, familiar with my performances for Dukla Holloway in helping guide them to the North London Invitation League championship title (1992–93). Word gets around. And, thinking about it, how would I feel, having unleashed one of my scorchers, to see the index finger of the country's top goalkeeper hanging limp at a ninety-degree angle?

'What about Alex Manninger?' I tried.

Bob had told me the week before that Manninger, the Arsenal reserve goalkeeper, would be a shoo-in if Seaman didn't like the idea.

'Same thing,' said Bob. 'I don't think you'll get any professional keeper who's willing to do it. Sorry. Good luck with the book.'

I later phoned Seaman's business agent, his wife, to see if he'd have a word with me about the art of saving penalties. She told me that he would prefer not to, because at some time in the future he planned to do his own book on penalties. In which case, I feel it is only fair that I take the opportunity right now to state, without bitterness, that I shall not be available to take penalties when he needs a journalist to test him.

I'd wanted to take on Seaman for obvious reasons: because he was the England goal-keeper in the last two tournaments that ended in shoot-outs and, it appeared, he would maintain that position in the next tournament, Euro 2000. He is also a very fine penalty-saver. But not necessarily the best penalty-saver. Statistically, that award would have to go to Mark Crossley, now of Middlesborough, and at the time reserve keeper at Nottingham Forest. A thirty-one-year-old goalkeeper who has not benefited from the most consistent good fortune in his career, Crossley has nevertheless enjoyed what might seem the luck only to have faced thirteen penalties in the top flight – the old First Division, the Premier League and FA Cup. (At least, thirteen is all he can remember facing.) But the luck resides with all those players who have never had to attempt to beat him from the spot. Of his thirteen penalties, he has saved eight. That's almost a sixty-five per cent record, over double the average of Premier-ship goalkeepers. In the 1998–1999 season, when Forest were relegated, he saved four out of five. Those figures don't include penalty shoot-outs, in which his ratio is three saves out of four penalties: seventy-five per cent. And they were not racked up against any old duffers. He's saved penalties from, among others: David Platt, which is not something he liked to mention, given that Platt was then his manager; Teddy Sheringham, Benito Carbone and Gary Lineker. He saved against Lineker in the 1991 FA Cup final, becoming, after his current teammate Dave Beasant, only the second goalkeeper ever to save a penalty at that stage of the competition at Wembley. Although he disagrees, he carries an even greater feat in his catalogue of penalty saves. A few seasons back, he made one against Matthew Le Tissier.

Le Tissier has taken forty-nine penalties so far in his time as a pro, and he has scored forty-eight of them. He is the Tiger Woods and Michael Jordan of penalties rolled into one magnificently efficient scoring machine. Almost halfway through his tally, in March 1993, when his total stood at twenty-one, he came up against Crossley at the Dell. 'I remember thinking that I wasn't going to save it,' Crossley told me. That reaction was uncharacteristic. One of the things I like about the Forest keeper is that he thinks penalty-takers should always score. Another thing I warm to is his conviction that goalkeepers should always assume they're going to save.

Initially, the word from Forest was that Crossley would talk but he wouldn't stand in goal for me. As a precautionary measure I faxed every club in the Premier League to request the services of their goalkeepers for ten penalty kicks. Four – Sunderland, Coventry, Everton and Watford – replied, but only Everton agreed, and then informed me that none of their goalkeepers was available until after my copy deadline. The fax-around turned out to be as precautionary as a split condom. And, as I was discovering, you could grow old and die before most people in football returned your phone calls. In desperation, I called the agent of a former England goalkeeper who was now comfortably middle-aged. I'd been told that the agent arranged penalty sessions for businessmen to try their luck against the one-time England number one. 'Ten penalties?' he repeated in a voice that sounded like it was clothed in a cheap suit. 'Yeah, well, we could do that. You're looking at fifteen hundred pounds. Or maybe we could arrange a deduction for a joint deal with the book and a share of the profits.'

I then I spoke to Crossley. Open, down-to-earth, interested and helpful, he was a revelation. Tentatively, I mentioned the niggling problem of theory having the edge over practice in my book. 'Well, if you can come up to the training ground,' said Crossley, 'you can take a few pens with me.'

I had a week to get ready. I worked out a preparatory programme that was designed, right down to the finest detail, to deliver success. The first step, I decided, was to buy a pair of football boots and a football. Before I could initiate my plan, however, I received the call that I had been waiting for. Some months after my request, Gary Lineker's agent – or, as it turned out, his agent's assistant – informed me that the 'Match of the Day' presenter would talk to me. Sometime in the next week. I was by now experienced in the labyrinthine procedures that tend to preface actual telephonic communication with footballers or ex-footballers – the anonymous intermediaries, the trails of cellular numbers, the broken promises – and which afford them the necessary protection from cranks like myself who are not offering money.

The Lineker deal was relatively simple. I just had to wait for his phone call. Lineker was that rare breed, an instinctive goalscorer who also analysed the game. I knew that he had gained a buzz out of taking penalties, and I was looking forward to discussing his ideas and memories. After the first day's fruitless telephone vigil, I briefly stepped out to deliver the bulk of the overdue manuscript. I wasn't too worried, because Lineker had my mobile number. However, when I returned to my office, there was a message from the former England striker, saying that he'd called and that he'd try again. I resolved not to leave the room for the rest of the week. He obviously wasn't going to mess around with the mobile. The afternoons I had set aside to practise penalties in the park were spent waiting by a phone. I didn't even dare go out to buy the football boots. After a few days of listening to the phone not ring, I began to feel like an obsessive stalker – albeit one who was uniquely passive and hopelessly incompetent. Lineker's agent's assistant was no longer taking my calls. I had to try to find out what was happening from his agent's assistant's assistant, until he called me a 'nuisance'. By the end of the week, I recognised that I had plumbed a tragic new level of celebrity-inspired delusion. I had merely persuaded myself that I was waiting for a call from Lineker. But why focus my psychosis on a man who, without wishing to be unkind, is hardly a superstar? Why didn't I simply choose to believe it was Madonna who was not phoning? In theory, after all, the phone call I was not receiving was just as likely not placed by Gwyneth Paltrow or, I don't know, Robert Mugabe as Lineker. Next week, I realised, I could wait for Luciano Pavarotti not to get in touch. The possibilities were endless. But the call from Lineker never came and in the end I only just managed to get a pair of boots before I boarded the train to Nottingham.

This is where it all began, in Nottingham. Every schoolboy used to know that Notts County is the world's oldest club, founded in 1862, long before an Irish goalkeeper fixated on the penalty kick. I had also known for years that only the River Trent separated the two stadiums of County and Forest from one another. Yet is was still a surprise to see how narrow the Trent is at this point, like a canal rather than a river. If you walk for about ten minutes along the towpath on the south side from the City Ground stadium, you come to Nottingham Forest's training ground, or at least the area they use for training. I didn't take the towpath, a mistake that would cause me severe distress later on. Instead I crossed the park from the other side and was pleased to see a figure I recognised as Mark Crossley diving about a goal not far from the perimeter fence. I stood outside and watched. My football boots were in my bag, ready for action, and I had already changed into a pair of tracksuit bottoms so as not to waste time when the moment came. Mark had asked me not to approach him if 'the boss' was around, so I decided not to bring my presence to his attention until I was sure that David Platt was not close by.

Having assured myself that the manager was a good half a mile away across the other side of the multi-pitch training area, I was about to gesture towards Mark when I suddenly heard a teammate call him 'Norm'. So this wasn't Crossley? Jesus, I thought, they have another keeper who's a dead ringer. How confusing. Perhaps I had misheard. But, no, everyone was calling him Norm. I tried a couple of waves but received no response.

Now I was in something of a quandary. Should I walk over to the other end of the pitch and look for another Crossley? What if there was no other Crossley? The training session was due to end any minute and the original Crossley might have gone by the time I made it back to him. I decided to stick with this Crossley and see what happened. He made a couple of superb saves during a five-a-side game, flying through the air and bending the ball round the post. What a majestic site. 'Great save, Norm,' said one of the coaches.

As I bent down to put my boots on, I went over what Francis Lee had told me about the spot kick. Lee took fifteen penalties for Manchester City in 1971–72 and scored all of them, a record that still stands. 'The first thing is,' he had said, 'you've got to want to take one.' I felt that, almost by definition, I passed that test. Why else had I spent two hours on a train from London? 'The next thing is,' Lee had continued, 'you've got to make your mind up before you hit the ball.' As I was planning to take ten penalties, I thought I'd wait until each individual shot, otherwise I was sure I'd forget the running order of decisions. He also suggested keeping the head down: 'You can hear it when it goes in.' And he preferred a long run-up because he thought a short one 'showed the goalie too much.' I couldn't see that, but still, he was the one with the fifteen out of fifteen score. That said, he'd also missed penalties, including the only two he took for England. 'Everyone misses,' he told me, philosophically.

His main worry had been muddy or heavy surfaces on which the standing foot could give way. In the 1970 European Cup Winners' Cup final, he had almost missed a penalty, which turned out to be the decider, when his left foot slipped. And playing for England against Portugal at Wembley, a few days after the Horse of the Year Show, his standing foot got stuck in the quagmire. 'I hit it that wide,' said Lee, of the resulting shot, 'I didn't just miss the post. I missed the photographers as well.'

The day was crisp and cloudless but, looking down at the turf, I noted with alarm that it was chewed up and soft from the previous night's rain. I then looked up and noted with even greater alarm that Mark or Norm or whoever he was had gone. The session was over and the players were walking across the pitches away from where I was standing. I slipped effortlessly and immediately into absolute panic. 'Mark!' I shouted six or seven times, but he couldn't hear me. He was either too far away or not Mark or both. I ran round the top of the perimeter to where I thought the entrance would be. But when I got there, I came up against a barrier of razor wire. That meant I would now have to run around three sides of the vast playing fields, which were about half the size of Nottinghamshire. The only exercise I had endured for the previous three months was turning on the computer each morning with my middle finger. For some reason, I was also wearing two coats, as well as carrying my kit bag.

What seemed like a month but may have been as little as four or five hours later, I was on the towpath, skidding precariously on my studs. I could see Mark or Norm a couple of hundred yards up ahead. I wanted to shout, but that would have required breath and energy and was therefore an impossibility. Instead I let out a high-pitched whine, like that of a domestic animal in need of feeding. Luckily the guy walking with Mark/Norm must have possessed the hearing of bat, because he drew his companion's attention to the disturbing noise. Bent over, and intimate with death, I raised a defeated arm. The goalkeeper looked momentarily baffled. Even now I dread to imagine what thoughts flickered across his mind as he looked back at this contorted figure with two coats, panting by the side of the river. Anyhow, he came back and shook my hand. It was Crossley. I learned later that Norm was a nickname given to him years ago by Stuart Pearce on account of a supposed resemblance to Norman Whiteside, the former Manchester United midfielder of celebrated hardness and legendary thirst. The name stuck, as it would if Psycho gave it you.

'Right then,' he said. 'Are you ready to do it now?'

What I was ready for was an oxygen tent and a glucose drip.

'Yeah,' I gasped, 'great.'

We returned to the training field. There was a handful of players collecting balls and messing around. Effectively the place was empty. But as Lineker once said: 'It's not about the crowd, it's about the technique.' Crossley stood in the goal, a forbidding presence, although not one that appeared impassable. I decided to put the first one high up to his left. What I intended to do was bring my right foot across the ball so that it would look, at first, as if I were aiming for his right. Crossley didn't dive, he just leaned the wrong way. The ball went exactly where I wanted it to. One-nil to me. For the next one, I thought I'd try the opposite: low down to his right. Crossley went the right way this time but I tucked the ball firmly in the corner.

I felt as if I were holding a banjo and had been instructed to hit a donkey's arse. I couldn't miss. I was even starting to breathe like a human again. As a matter of fact, I began to feel a little guilty. Here was this guy, a top-rate professional, a master of his trade, who had kindly taken the time at the end of a training session to indulge my arcane request while he could have been enjoying a hot shower, and what did I do? I came on like a big-shot, like a show-off, like a winner.

'Are you going for ten out of ten, then?' asked Mark.

Of course I was. Then a strange thing happened. I didn't know where to aim the ball. I had run out of ideas already. Each time I though of an area of the goal, it seemed obvious and I selected another. Crossley had somehow imposed himself on the space. He didn't seem to do anything. Paul Cooper, the former Ipswich Town goalkeeper, developed a technique of standing slightly to one side, his weaker side, and subtly daring the taker to go for the larger space. He saved eight out of ten penalties that way in 1979–80. Crossley just stood there in the middle with his head straight, feet not too far apart and arms ready.

As I ran up, I sensed that I had psyched myself out or had been psyched out in some inexplicably devious way by Crossley, and I blasted the ball. It sailed over the bar, as if it were an ironic homage to Waddle's Turin effort. I had gone from super-confidence to wretched despair inside a few seconds. The answer, I reasoned, was to place the next shot as carefully as possible. No matter if it was easy to read, it would be too difficult to reach. I hit the ball with my instep and went for just inside his left post. I got just outside the left post, a small but crucial difference. Two-all. I was cracking.

The fifth shot was a miss-hit. My standing foot, my left foot, got caught and I scuffed the ball to Crossley's right as he moved left. It was the perfect penalty as defined by no less an authority than Le Tissier. 'The perfect penalty', he has sagaciously declared, 'is one that hits the back of the net.' Mine just about qualified.

I don't know what went wrong with the sixth. I suppose the straightforward answer is, *everything*. Afterwards I tried to convince myself that I had deliberately hit the ball down the middle, but I'm fairly certain that I had another part of the goal in mind; specifically, one of the corners. Crossley didn't move. He stood his ground and welcomed the ball at chest-height in grateful arms.

'You see,' he said, perhaps a touch unnecessarily, 'that wouldn't have happened in a match. I would have dived.'

The reason he didn't dive was because I wasn't striking the ball hard enough. 'No disrespect,' he gently added, 'but you're not a pro and that makes a difference.' He then came out of the goal and demonstrated how a professional footballer kicks the ball. His action was charged yet smooth. The ball flew into the bottom-right corner. It was as if someone had speeded up the film. Crossley, it transpires, is something of a penalty-taking specialist. He took one in the shoot-out against Chelsea in a pre-season Umbro Cup tournament and scored. He'd like to take them more often.

I realised, a little forlornly, that Crossley had not really dived on any of my shots. We spoke a little about how in match conditions he anticipated which way to go. The run-up was important. He followed the same established clues: if it was straight on for a right-footed player, then most often he would put the ball to Crossley's right. And if the right-footed player came from the left, he usually placed it in the other corner. In tight games, he thought, players were inclined to hit across the ball, so that the right-footer would go for the keeper's right side. He said that with someone like Matthew Elliot, whom he has never faced, he would simply stand in the middle. 'He hits it straight and hard, about eighty miles per hour. You would just hope that he put it inside what goalkeepers call their cage, the space immediately around you that you can reach with your arms. You should always save in your cage. But at eighty miles per hour outside: no chance.'

Crossley does his homework on the opposition's penalty-taker a couple of days before a game. He waits until seeing the run-up, though, before deciding which way to go. I asked him what other clues he looked for, but he said he wasn't conscious of them. 'It's like changing gears in your car. When do you go from second to third? You don't think about it, you instinctively know.'

Research has shown that there are a series of pointers, beginning with the angle of run-up and ending with point-of-ball contact, that become progressively more reliable leading up to the kick. Of course, the problem is that the later the keeper leaves it to decide, the less time he has to react. Unless the ball is hit poorly (see my sixth penalty), point-of-ball contact is too late. A paper produced by academics from the University of British Columbia, suggests that the compromise clue is the position of the non-kicking foot prior to contact: basically the ball goes in whatever direction the non-kicking foot is pointed. This sign is late enough in the movement to be eighty per cent reliable, but still allows time to respond.

There is another variable that remains the subject of much disagreement in scientific circles, and that is the question of reaction time. Until relatively recently, it was widely agreed that human reaction time was between 0.1 and 0.2 seconds (i.e., 100 to 200 milliseconds). The International Amateur Athletic

Federation, for example, sets the time of 100 milliseconds after a starting pistol as the earliest time that a sprinter can set off without being disqualified for cheating (as Linford Christie was at the Atlanta Olympics in 1996 when he went off after 80 milliseconds).

A study by the Medical Research Council's Human Movement and Balance Unit in London showed that in normal circumstances we respond to stimuli via the cerebral cortex, a process that takes as long as 200 milliseconds. But when provoked, for instance, by an unexpected noise, the reaction time was shortened to as little as 60 milliseconds. The involuntary reaction is much faster because the 'startle reflex', a primitive circuit that by-passes the cerebral cortex and was designed to respond to trouble, kicks in. A number of scientists have speculated that some athletes may be able, unconsciously, to plug into this startle reflex by psyching themselves up. Crossley told me that before each penalty, he turned his back to the spot and said to himself: 'Come on! You can save this.' Sometimes he didn't even need to rev himself up, he could tell by looking at the player twelve yards away that he wasn't up to the task. 'You can see when they don't fancy it,' he said.

I COULD DO THAT

All of which, as far as I could see, meant that I needed to look the part and hit the ball harder. With Crossley back in goal and no doubt telling himself that he was going to save it, I went on a bold Franny Lee run-up. Lee claims that he used to hit the ball at three-quarter speed, as if he were making a fifty- or sixty-yard pass. I went for full speed, which, translated to Lee's capability, was probably about one-quarter speed. Did I keep my head down? I thought so. Having said that, I clearly saw the ball rise over the crossbar and off into the distance. The fifty- or sixty-yard pass I had certainly managed. My only error was not to have made sure that the 192-square-foot target intervened.

Mark, a charmingly understated character who displayed little of the eccentricity for which goalkeepers are renowned, gave me a consoling smile. Four-three to him. My eighth penalty was unquestionably the most satisfying. I felt as though I really had to score, and yet I didn't go for pace. Instead I stroked the ball, without looking at it, to the keeper's left. My eyes were fixed on Crossley until I flashed them to his right and sent him that way as well. He noticed. 'That's the first time you haven't looked at the ball.'

151

ON PENALTIES

Eric Cantona and Le Tissier seldom looked at the ball, preferring to keep their gaze on the goalkeeper, to see where he moved in time to adjust. My next shot was also reminiscent of a Le Tissier penalty, his twenty-second to be precise, the one Crossley saved. They were pretty much identical, as was Mark's electric dive, the only fully-fledged dive he made against me. Although a firm shot, it was not close enough to the post and Mark anticipated its flight, moving flat-out, mid-air, to his left. There is a gloriously acrobatic gracefulness to this kind of save. It seems so aesthetically correct that you almost want to place the ball in that area (about three feet above the ground and six feet in from the post) to make the keeper look good. Perhaps Le Tissier was admiring the elegance of man meeting ball when Crossley saved his penalty. Or perhaps he was simply surprised that his twenty-second spot kick had been saved. Either way, when the ball rebounded off Crossley's palms and back into this path, Le Tissier skied it over an open goal.

The last penalty. I had to convert it to level the scores. I gave it all I had. Mark got his hand to it just outside his cage and about a foot beneath the bar. The ball went in. Did he give it to me? I'd like to think not, but he told me afterwards that if a keeper gets his hand to ball he should never let it go in. Five-all. What did it all prove? In the scientific sense, nothing. It may, I suppose, have confirmed what was already known, that Crossley is a very fine goalkeeper and that I write words for a living. Even so, I feel that, had I taken or found the time to practise, I would have done better. Perhaps Crossley would have then tried harder, but that would have been an achievement in itself. Ultimately, it underlined the curious duality of the penalty. It is an easy way to score a goal but also a complex way to miss one. And the two are frequently no more than inches apart. Nevertheless, my own suspicion, as I've tiresomely repeated, is that practice, while not an infallible approach, can only help make that distance greater. If I am guilty of over-emphasising the point, it's because I don't want to endure another experience like 1990, 1996 and 1998. When I asked, the FA told me that Kevin Keegan had no special view on penalties other than that it is 'impossible to recreate match conditions in training'.

As luck and tactical naivety would have it, that dread line of thinking was not put to the test in Euro 2000. England went out before the knock-out stage, although once more the victims of the penalty. This time it was the 89th minute spot-kick conceded, clumsily, by Phil Neville in the final group match against Romania. It took an ignominious exit such as this to remind us how glorious defeat in a shoot-out could seem. Suddenly the 1990s was a closed era and the nearly nights, with all their beautiful and terrible drama, were a thing of the past. Now that England were so far from victory you could see how close they had once come. Now those three penalty shoot-outs, which had been a source of endless frustration, could become the subject of soothing nostalgia.

I doubt the Dutch are yet ready to see things that way. Their semi-final against Italy was the showdown between the two worst penalty-taking sides in the world, including England. Whoever lost would claim the undisputed, and unwanted, title of foremost international incompetents from 12 yards. The Dutch played the best football in the tournament but I fancied them to come second in the shoot-out. Having already missed two penalties in open play against Italy, they had what it took to lose: a fear of winning. For the shoot-out offers the ultimate

means of not winning, without really losing.
The Netherlands have historically fallen at the
final hurdle (the brilliant 1970s side lost two
world cup finals against inferior teams) and
there is no more final hurdle than the penalty
shoot-out. In Dutch football mythology
victory seems almost to spoil the purity of
their play and, in that sense, they have made a
philosophical accommodation with defeat.
The English too have grown comfortable with
the prospect of not winning. Deep down, I
suspect, that's why penalty practice has been
avoided, because it keeps open the option of
honourable defeat.

From where English football stands currently, somewhere between grim hope and
resigned humiliation, we can only dream of
the exotica of the penalty shoot-out. But if
England should find themselves lining up for
one any time soon, it would be nice to think
that this time they were prepared for a victory
that carries its own special honour.